WHAT'S MY TEENAGER THINKING?

DK

WHAT'S MY TEENAGER THINKING?

PRACTICAL CHILD PSYCHOLOGY FOR MODERN PARENTS

TANITH CAREY

COUNSELING PSYCHOLOGIST
DR. CARL PICKHARDT

Penguin
Random
House

Senior Editor	Claire Cross
US Editor	Kayla Dugger
US Executive Editor	Lori Hand
Senior Art Editor	Emma Forge
Senior Designer	Tom Forge
Editorial Assistant	Kiron Gill
Illustrator	Céleste Wallaert
Senior Producer, Pre-production	Tony Phipps
Senior Producer	Luca Bazzoli
Senior Jacket Designer	Nicola Powling
Jacket Co-ordinator	Lucy Philpott
Creative Technical Support	Tom Morse
Managing Editor	Dawn Henderson
Managing Art Editor	Marianne Markham
Art Director	Maxine Pedliham
Publishing Director	Mary-Clare Jerram

The views expressed in this book are the author's own. The information in this book has been compiled as general guidance on the specific subjects addressed. It is not a substitute and not to be relied on for medical, healthcare, or pharmaceutical professional advice. If you have any concerns about any aspect of your child's behavior, health, or well-being, please seek professional advice. Please seek medical advice before changing, stopping, or starting any of your child's medical treatment. So far as the author is aware, the information given is correct and up to date as of May 2020. Practice, laws, and regulations all change and the reader should obtain up-to-date professional advice on any such issues. The author and publishers disclaim, as far as the law allows, any liability arising directly or indirectly from the use or misuse of the information contained in this book.

First American Edition, 2020
Published in the United States by DK Publishing
1450 Broadway, Suite 801, New York, NY 10018

Copyright © 2020 Dorling Kindersley Limited
DK, a Division of Penguin Random House LLC
20 21 22 23 24 10 9 8 7 6 5 4 3 2 1
001–314919–Jun/2020

A catalog record for this book
is available from the Library of Congress.
ISBN 978-1-4654-9232-6

Printed and bound in Latvia
All images © Dorling Kindersley Limited
For further information see: www.dkimages.com

A WORLD OF IDEAS:
SEE ALL THERE IS TO KNOW
www.dk.com

CONTENTS

CHAPTER 3

Your 15–16-year-old

CHAPTER 4

Your 17–18-year-old

FOREWORD

For parents at a loss for how to anticipate, understand, and react to common adolescent changes during the teenage years, this helpful book provides an episodic sampling of many encounters likely to occur, along with realistic preparation and practical, research-based advice.

"Picture this," each episodic illustration seems to say. With that visual in mind, the reader is then led into a verbal explanation of the behavior going on and the dynamics at play, followed by specific suggestions for what parents might effectively do or say. *This book can help parents by being both descriptive and prescriptive.*

Even when the suggested explanation and response aren't entirely applicable, the author's ideas can clarify the reader's thinking about their individual family situation. This is as it should be. Because of its extraordinary complexity, parenting remains more of an art than a science. Similar as they may look, each parent-teenager relationship is unique. Not every encounter described by the author will occur in all families. *This book can help parents by honoring the reality that there is enormous variation in the adolescent passage.*

The function of a young person's adolescence is to differentiate and detach from childhood and family to develop a fitting individuality and a functional independence. Now parents have two jobs to do: First, create and express a stable family structure of responsible rules and expectations for their teenager to grow up within. Second, stay caringly connected to their growing daughter or son as adolescence gradually pushes them apart, which it is meant to do. *This book can act as a communication manual, enabling parents to bridge normal differences with their teenager as adolescent growth unfolds.*

Some parenting books are meant to be studied all the way through to be useful, but this one does not need to be read in its entirety to be helpful; it is written for browsing. *This book can help parents by being a resource when searching for topical information that fits their current interest and concern.*

When I counsel with parents about their adolescents, I use "scripting" a lot. Curious parents frequently ask, "What can I say to my teenager about this?" Such assistance is often valued by parents who otherwise feel at a loss for words. *This book can help parents by suggesting speech to specifically address their concerns in a way the young person can hear.*

The content of this book answers the question posed by the title: *What Is My Teenager Thinking?* Reading it helps parents become more sensitive to the adolescent experience and mindset, which the young person can appreciate: "At least I feel understood!" *This book can help parents be more understanding and empathetic.*

In addition to demanding dedication of love and assumption of responsibility, parenting an adolescent is an ongoing process of adjustment in which the mother or father must continually play catch-up to their evolving teenager. *This book can help parents keep their expectations ahead of the growth curve, anticipating normal changes so they are not blindsided when the latest adolescent alteration occurs.*

So you are in for a treat. Not all self-help books are that helpful, but this one is.

DR. CARL PICKHARDT
PhD, Counseling Psychologist
Psychology Today blogger: *Surviving (Your Child's) Adolescence*

CHAPTER 1

UNDERSTANDING THE
TEENAGE
YEARS

YOUR OWN
TEENAGE YEARS

We remember our teenage years vividly. From our first kiss to passing our driver's test, these memories tend to feel especially meaningful. But our teens are not us, and to parent in the present, first we may need to make sense of our past.

If certain types of teenage behavior trigger irrational responses in you, figuring out why can help you adjust your reactions. For example, all teens disobey parents occasionally as part of the process of becoming independent. If your parents had a "Do as I say" authoritarian parenting style, you may carry forward the belief that adults should always be obeyed, or veer the other way and be much more lax. If a parent shamed, used the silent treatment, or dismissed your feelings and you've never processed this treatment, these reactions can become your default setting at times of conflict or stress with your teen. Or if difficult friendships or academic disappointments were a feature of your adolescence, you may find you're sensitive when your teen encounters similar issues.

Look back at your childhood and ask yourself these questions:

◉ What do you like or dislike about the way your parents brought you up?

◉ In three words, how would you describe your relationship as a teenager with your parents?

◉ What impact has the way you were parented as a teenager had on the adult you?

Now look at the present:

◉ Is there a behavior that your teen adopts that makes you see red?

◉ Why do you think this issue provokes you? Does it link back to treatment you received?

◉ Think of times you've labeled your teenager's behavior and recall whether you or a sibling were ever labeled similarly and how that felt.

Mindful parenting

If you have a co-parent, share memories and thoughts. Compare experiences and agree on the best ways to support each other and to parent your teen. Letting go of some of the ways you were parented won't happen overnight. No parent gets it right all the time.

The important thing is to start noticing patterns of unhelpful beliefs and biases. Look out for these signs:

⊚ Check for inner voices telling you how your teen "should" or "ought" to act without considering context or circumstance.

⊚ Watch out for a tendency to give generalized labels, such as "lazy," "spoiled," or "bratty."

⊚ Notice times when your teenager's behavior makes you physically tense. This may be a sign that the primal, reactive part of your brain has been triggered, overcoming logical thinking.

⊚ When considering your teen's behavior, watch out for catastrophic thinking—images that flash into your mind imagining him or her failing or having a disastrous future.

Gaining perspective

Adolescents can be reactive because they're learning to regulate their emotions. If you lose control, too, and stereotype your teen, conflicts can escalate. To keep a sense of perspective, ask yourself, "How does my teen usually feel about himself after he's spent time with me?" and "How do I want him to describe my parenting in 20 years' time?"

❝ ❞

REEVALUATING YOUR ADOLESCENCE CAN STOP YOU FROM UNCONSCIOUSLY REPEATING PATTERNS.

YOUR TEENAGER'S **BRAIN**

Though the brain is almost adult size at the onset of puberty, its internal wiring is only about 80 percent finished. The process of completing the final 20 percent starts when the frontal lobe increases in density—around the time that adolescence begins.

Brain development in the teenage years

It takes until the mid-twenties for the frontal lobe, the area responsible for the executive functions of reasoning, judgment, self-control, and planning, to link up fully to other parts of the brain.

Over the next few years, this involves two processes. The first is that axons—the long, thin tendrils that stretch between nerve cells and carry information—become coated with an insulating, fatty substance known as myelin. Called myelination, this strengthens and speeds up communication, allowing neuronal messages to travel thousands of times faster and integrating both sides of the brain so that thinking becomes more sophisticated. The other process is the pruning back of brain cells that aren't used or needed, increasing the brain's efficiency.

Both of these processes happen at different times in different parts of the brain, with the prefrontal cortex the last part of your teen's brain to be connected. This means that the counterbalancing thoughts your teen needs to regulate emotions don't travel quickly enough to head off impulsive behavior. Instead of taking stock, she's more likely to rush in without considering the consequences.

Research also reveals another reason why teens experience the world differently than adults. In adolescence, the nucleus accumbens—a mass of neurons sometimes called the "pleasure center"—grows to its largest size, fueled in part by higher levels of the feel-good chemical dopamine. This adds to the hit that comes from adventure. All of this means that nothing ever feels quite as good as it does when you're an adolescent—and the rewards of taking risks feel all the greater.

The part played by hormones

So what about hormones—often blamed for erratic teen behavior? While the rise in sexual hormones certainly increases and triggers changes in your teen's body—and creates sexual

" "
WHILE THEIR BRAINS DEVELOP, TEENS ARE WIRED FOR THRILLS AND RISK-TAKING.

feelings—it's more likely that brain changes are behind teens' mood swings. However, stress hormones such as cortisol do make the primal and emotional brain and its antennae for threat, the amygdala, more sensitive. This means that stress hormones trigger the fight-or-flight response more quickly and intensely because the prefrontal cortex isn't fully wired yet.

The message for parents
Understanding this cognitive development can enhance your communication. Knowing that logic and planning are a challenge for your teen can help you resist the urge to "nag"—likely to make her either tune out or to fire up a defensive fight-or-flight response—and instead support, guide, and listen. The upside of her rapidly changing brain is she's a good learner. When you lead her to more reasonable responses, over time, these become her internal conscience, enabling her to make wiser, thoughtful decisions.

NAVIGATING
THE TEENAGE YEARS

The modern world throws up many new challenges for teenagers, but the good news is that advances in our understanding of the teenage brain mean we can use this insight to help our teens thrive.

Thanks to scanning technology, which shows how parts of the brain light up in response to stimuli, we can see it in action and how it gradually links up. Your teen will naturally learn lessons from discovering the consequences of his actions. Understanding what drives his behavior can help you guide him. As he navigates the world, think of yourself as an encouraging life coach. When he encounters failure or hurt, letting him express his thoughts will help him use the left- and right-hand sides and lower- and higher-thinking parts of his brain so he can fully process experiences.

Recognizing progress
You won't see when he's made a cognitive leap. His progress won't be as clear as when he first crawled or spoke. But when you see him master frustration and anger, persevere with tasks he might have dismissed as too hard weeks before, set longer-term goals, and consider others' views, you'll know he's moving in the right direction.

THE EARLY TEENAGE YEARS
YOUR 13–14-YEAR-OLD

Your teen is figuring out who he is and which group of peers he belongs to, but he still heavily relies on your support. Brain rewiring and hormonal surges can lead to rash actions.

How your teen thinks

⊚ His thinking is black and white—he tends to believe things are "right" or "wrong." Abstract thinking is challenging, but he'll gradually expand his intellectual interests and switch more easily between ideas.

How your teen feels

⊚ The tendency to compare himself to others peaks now. Consequently, self-esteem and confidence may dip.

⊚ He feels acutely sensitive to being "watched," even when no peers are present. This means he's highly self-conscious if he or anyone connected to him does something he believes others will judge.

⊚ A crush is likely now as he gets a "dopamine squirt"—the release of the neurotransmitter dopamine, which sends a rush of pleasure to the brain's reward systems—when he sees someone he's attracted to.

⊚ His belief that he's uniquely special and therefore invulnerable to danger, known as "the personal fable," is highest now.

How your teen acts

⊚ The brain's reorganization, the insecurity created by puberty, and the need to belong mean he may have a temporary achievement dip, particularly if his peer group consider that working hard is uncool.

⊚ Rising testosterone levels in all genders are linked not only to an increase in sexual desire, but also a drive for social status and risk-taking. As the brain's executive functions of self-control are still being wired, he may "crash" into situations that look entirely preventable to you.

⊚ He's highly egocentric, believing others are as fascinated by him as he is with himself. He finds it hard to see the world from others' perspectives, so he can be self-centered and lack empathy.

⊚ Cliquiness and social conflict is at its highest now, and your teen and his peers are ruthless about seeking and maintaining social status.

THE MID-TEENAGE YEARS
YOUR 15–16-YEAR-OLD

Your teen's cognitive and analytical skills become more refined as the brain continues to develop. With friendships cementing, she's more self-assured but is still impulsive and takes risks.

How your teen thinks

⊚ A process known as synaptogenesis—the growth of brain connections—as well as the pruning of unused brain cells means that her brain is becoming more specialized and efficient. She finds it easier to excel in certain areas, whether in sports or a subject, creating a stronger sense of identity.

⊚ Planning skills increase, and she starts to set goals for her future, which she sees as a place of fun and freedom.

⊚ She thinks more about the meaning of life and her role in the world. She's weighing her morals and her family's values.

⊚ She's grasping that knowledge isn't absolute and there isn't always just one right answer.

How your teen feels

⊚ She may move toward mixed-gender groups and welcome the different ways people of other genders and orientations think and behave.

⊚ Unless there are friendship issues that she needs support with, she's likely to feel increasingly comfortable with peers, who she believes understand her best. She'll exert her growing independence by spending more time with, and putting more store in the opinions of, her friends.

⊚ She's likely to be forming strong ideas about her sexual orientation, even though she may still be exploring different aspects. This is the age when LGBTQ+ teens are most likely to come out to parents.

How your teen acts

⊚ With her physical development almost complete, she may want to experiment with identities and looks.

⊚ The pull between peers, family, and school responsibilities can mean she's more argumentative and defiant. However, her growing control over her impulses means she's less likely to lash out and more likely to withdraw in an argument.

⊚ She's likely to question rules and authority and why others have power over her.

THE LATE TEENAGE YEARS
YOUR 17–18-YEAR-OLD

*Your teen's thinking is increasingly rational and balanced.
His increased maturity and ability to empathize help
bring you closer.*

How your teen thinks

◉ Metacognition—the ability to understand his thought processes—is well developed now. He foresees consequences better and grasps how much work and time tasks such as homework will take.

◉ The continued wiring of the prefrontal cortex means he responds more calmly and logically to stressful situations. Aggression and mood swings start to decrease.

How your teen feels

◉ Unless there's been a trauma or rift, he'll become closer and more respectful to you. He'll also feel more comfortable seeking advice and talking about personal issues.

◉ He has a more accurate idea of what he needs to do to achieve goals. After idealizing the future, he may become more nervous about the realities and responsibilities of adult life.

◉ Peer pressure no longer exerts such a pull as he develops a stronger sense of who he is and what he believes—he'll find it easier to decline risky behavior.

How your teen acts

◉ He has a clear moral compass and may want to take part in activities that show his conviction, such as demonstrations or volunteering.

◉ He may have a serious romantic relationship now. By the time they graduate from high school, half of teens have had sex.

◉ He's more able to see the world from others' perspectives and will tend to behave in less selfish, more thoughtful ways.

ENJOYING LIFE WITH
YOUR TEENAGER

Although adolescence is still often talked about as a period to be "survived" by teens and "put up with" by parents, recent findings on psychological development and in neuroscience reveal what a creative and exciting time these years really are.

A period of positive change

As exasperating as they can sometimes be, teenagers behave as they do for good reason. Most of the behavior that adults find challenging has both an upside and an evolutionary purpose and also reflects the changes teenage brains must go through on the way to adulthood.

For example, you may believe your teen succumbs to peer pressure. In fact, she is wired to behave this way. Scans show she gets a bigger dopamine kick in her brain's pleasure center when she fits in with friends—and she's more likely to take risks in their company. Yet it's this wiring that also encourages her to move beyond the safe sphere of her family, explore the world, and find a new group to fit into.

Painful though conflict with your teen is, those regular fights also have a role. Teenagers can't become grown-ups without establishing some sort of separation from the dominant adults in their lives.

Listening to your teen

It's easy for parents to turn the adolescent years into a battle of wills. The temptation is to believe your teenager needs to change, not you, even though she's doing what she's meant to do. But if you're open to what she has to say, you can learn a lot from your child.

As she develops more sophisticated ways of thinking, she can point out some of the ironies you may have stopped seeing. Also, her curiosity about how the world works means she may spot injustices that you haven't noticed. With her forward-looking attitude, your teen has the optimism to want to improve the world, unclouded by some of the cynicism that might have crept into many adults' outlook.

You may find the intensity of her feelings scary sometimes. After all, she experiences emotions with fewer filters. But this is precisely why she's so passionate and excited about life—and why she fills your home with energy and laughter.

" "

YOUR TEENAGER'S ENERGY AND FORWARD-LOOKING ATTITUDE CAN REVITALIZE YOUR VIEW OF THE WORLD.

The rise of rolling news on social media means she's also informed on current issues. And with the autonomy that social media grants her, she's more able to stand up for her beliefs. Whether it's in areas such as the planet's welfare, animal rights, or gender equality, your teen can challenge your thinking—and ask you to join her in changing things for the better.

When you understand this important stage of her neurological development, you can start to appreciate the brilliance of her ever-changing brain. So find ways to enjoy her adolescence—laugh with her, ask her opinions, and value her unique blend of qualities. Bear in mind, the central goal of the teenage years has never been to make life difficult for parents. First and foremost, it has always been to become an independent adult with the skills to make her way in the world without you.

CHAPTER 2

YOUR
13 – 14
YEAR-OLD

"I'LL CLEAN MY ROOM IN A MINUTE."

When younger, your teenager used his room as a place to sleep and keep his things. Now he sees it as a personal expression of who he is. In his mind, not cleaning his room may also represent his freedom to start living life on his own terms.

SCENARIO | Your teen's room looks as if it's been hit by a bomb.

To your son, his bedroom is the one place that belongs just to him. As he gets older, it becomes a treasured sanctuary into which he can escape, process thoughts, relax, and have privacy. How he decorates it also provides a window into his interests. However, keeping it clean involves a level of planning and self-discipline that he struggles with while his brain is developing. You may see chaos, but he sees a place to enjoy his possessions, however they're arranged.

WHAT YOU MIGHT BE THINKING

You may be concerned and frustrated by his disorganization and by how he puts off your simple request to maintain basic levels of cleanliness. You may also feel like he shows a lack of respect for you and his belongings.

WHAT HE MIGHT BE THINKING

⊚ **The cognitive processes** in the frontal lobes of his brain are still developing, so he may not have the organization and planning abilities to keep on top of the mess. It's also possible that he genuinely doesn't see messiness in the way that you do, but as more of a comfort blanket.

⊚ **Your teen is coping** with increased academic and extracurricular pressures and may feel he doesn't have to keep his room neat, too.

⊚ **He's processing** lots of new information as he juggles his social life with academic demands. In this pressured phase, his room is a place to recuperate on his terms.

⊚ **He knows that cleanliness** is more important to you than it is to him. Not being as neat as you would like could be his subtle way of asserting independence. If he's feeling the weight of adult expectation in the only place that he feels is his, he may be pushing back.

SEE RELATED TOPICS
You always criticize: pp.148–149
I don't have time: pp.166–167

HOW YOU COULD RESPOND

In the moment

See it as a phase
You want to prepare your teen for the day when he'll have to live independently. He wants more autonomy but doesn't yet see cleanliness as a priority. Try to view messiness as part of the transition.

Talk about the advantages
Rather than make cleaning up feel like a punishment, point out the benefits. Is there a danger he could feel overwhelmed if he can't find things?

Appeal to a desire to look good
Point out that clothes look better when hung up or put away rather than getting wrinkled on the floor.

Break the task down
When faced with a big job, he may not know where to begin. Limit instructions to one or two. Perhaps give him a trash bag for waste, or put the laundry basket in his room so he can throw in dirty clothes. Suggest he vacuums his room while listening to a song to see the difference he can make in a few minutes.

Don't sweat the small stuff
As long as moldy food or damp clothes aren't creating a health hazard, allow him some control. Trust that he'll eventually work out that a cleaner room can be more pleasant.

In the long term

Don't overgeneralize
Resist the temptation to call him a slob because his room is messy. He may think you disapprove of him, not just of his room.

Let him choose the décor
If he feels the décor reflects his personal tastes, he's likely to be more invested in keeping his room looking relatively clean.

Think about storage
Most teens want to find the things they need quickly. Brainstorm storage solutions, such as putting up hooks to remove possessions from the floor.

Suggest a clean-out
Teens often hold onto childhood toys while acquiring new devices and clothes. Would he like a clean-out so he can move to the next stage of his life?

Look at it as a positive
Anxious teenagers are more likely to be obsessively clean, so see his messiness as a sign that he's relaxed enough to be himself at home.

"I NEED A NEW PHONE."

Fitting in and feeling liked are crucial for young teenagers. Your teenager is finding her way socially and forging new friendships. The objects she owns may help her "borrow" a feeling of belonging.

SCENARIO | Your teen complains that it's embarrassing to have an old phone.

For most children, getting a smartphone is a rite of passage when they start middle school. However, this sets off a competition over who has the latest model, fueled by phone companies releasing updated versions. Smartphones are also high end and easy to compare, and because teens constantly hold them, they're very visible. As a result, they're their number-one status symbol.

WHAT YOU MIGHT BE THINKING

You may feel you spend enough on her devices and phone bills without paying for upgrades. However, you may also worry that it looks like you can't afford to upgrade and that she'll feel humiliated in front of friends.

WHAT SHE MIGHT BE THINKING

◉ **Her phone may work** perfectly for the reason you gave it to her—so she could contact you if needed and vice versa. However, because she conducts her social life on it, having the latest model feels important to her. She may be frustrated and angry if she feels her older phone is slow, especially if she can't keep up as friends scroll through their feeds or her pictures won't load.

◉ **She may want** the latest phone to impress peers with slick images.

◉ **She's acutely sensitive** to social comparison. She may be worrying that friends think her family can't afford an update.

◉ **Teenagers tend to put** their needs first. She may think she needs a new model before you, even if your device is older.

SEE RELATED TOPICS
It's my phone: pp.96–97
Can I have next week's allowance?: pp.124–125

> **FITTING IN IS IMPORTANT FOR YOUR TEENAGER—THE OBJECTS SHE OWNS CAN BOOST HER FEELING OF BELONGING.**

HOW YOU COULD RESPOND

In the moment

Acknowledge her desires
Your first instinct may be to refuse, but this is likely to frustrate her more. Acknowledge her perspective. Say, "I can hear how much you want a new phone."

Check what her friends have
Teenagers can exaggerate. To gain perspective, ask how many of her friends have a new model—"everyone," or just one classmate?

Find out what she thinks is wrong
Teenagers tend to see the world in black and white. Is she writing off her phone because it lacks one feature? Does she need an entirely new model for this?

Talk about the advantages of older phones
Explain how a new phone increases her risk of being targeted for theft and that she'll worry about breaking it.

In the long term

Discuss status symbols
She may believe the latest phone will raise her popularity. Talk about how research shows teens are more comfortable with those who have the same level of possessions.

Help her manage photos
Thousands of photos slow phones down. Train her to delete photos to manage her phone storage.

Be a good role model
Moderate your need to buy the latest devices. Chat about where products come from, ethical trading, and the human and environmental cost of consumerism.

Suggest she earns it
If you give in to every demand, she'll take your generosity for granted. Instead, offer money toward a phone for her birthday or suggest ways to earn money.

"HOW TALL WILL I GET?"

In early adolescence, teenagers grow at different rates according to how far through puberty they are. Whether they look close to adult size or small for their age, teenagers can be sensitive about how they compare.

SCENARIO | Your teen has outgrown the pants and shoes you bought him only 3 months ago.

Between the ages of 12 and 15, boys grow on average 2¾–3½ in (7–9 cm) a year. On average, girls start growing 1 to 2 years earlier and can grow by up to 3¼ in (8 cm) a year, usually stopping 2 years after their first period, often around the age of 14. The hands and feet usually grow first, followed by the arms and legs, then the spine and torso. Finally, boys' chests expand while girls' hips widen. While teenagers' heights tend to even out eventually, at times there can be considerable disparity in growth rates. In your teen's mind, it's all about timing.

WHAT YOU MIGHT BE THINKING

When your teen matches or overtakes your height, it's a poignant milestone, causing you to take stock of how much he's changed. You may also fear that you'll lose authority. Conversely, you may worry if his growth is slow.

WHAT HE MIGHT BE THINKING

⊚ **He may be anxious** that he can't control his growth. Teenagers who shoot up may hunch their shoulders, alter their eating habits, or even stop eating protein in the false belief they'll grow less. Some may go to bed later because they think that most growth occurs while asleep.

⊚ **Because different parts** of his body grow before his brain has developed the spatial awareness to match the growth, this can make him clumsy. He may be hypersensitive and embarrassed.

⊚ **For boys especially**, height and mature physicality can be a social advantage. But while he may look grown up, he may still need emotional support. Smaller boys will need reassurance that heights usually even out.

⊚ **Shorter girls** may not be as worried because being small is often construed as "cute." If a girl is much taller than her friends, she may need reassuring that many peers will catch up or help with her posture and confidence so she feels comfortable being taller.

HOW YOU COULD RESPOND

In the moment

Treat him according to his age
Often, we let what we see override what we know. Even if he's physically well-developed for his age, emotionally he's still his chronological age.

Chat about what to expect
Talk about at what age you and his other biological parent hit puberty and your growth. Help him feel more in control by talking about his predicted height, which is usually his mother's and father's added heights, plus 5 in (13 cm), then the total divided by 2.

Put it in context
Show him pictures of you and your co-parent growing up to illustrate how growth happens in stages.

Tell him not to take advantage
Make it clear that now he's taller, you expect him to stick to the law on buying items such as alcohol.

Give him examples
Talk about public role models he knows who are physically different to their peers to reassure him that people are all shapes and sizes.

In the long term

Help him adjust
Talk about posture and gait. Even if he's shorter than his friends, how he stands and walks conveys maturity. If he's tall, encourage him to stand tall rather than stoop.

Don't label
However tall he is, don't keep referring to it or it will make him more self-conscious.

Encourage exercise
Exercise will help him develop the coordination and muscle strength needed to match bone growth.

Try to stay physically close
A hug may not feel quite the same now that you need to reach up to put your arms around him. Try a sideways hug or shoulder squeeze as he's sitting to show that you're still there to comfort and love him.

❝ ❞

TEENAGERS CAN BE HYPERSENSITIVE ABOUT THEIR GROWTH.

SEE RELATED TOPICS
I need a new bra: pp.60–61
I need some shaving stuff: pp.114–115

"THERE'S NOTHING TO EAT."

As teenagers begin to enjoy greater independence, they may start to buy more fast foods and candy with spending cash on their way to or from school—with the result that they turn their noses up at healthier basics at home.

SCENARIO | After school, your teen opens the fridge and loudly complains that there's nothing to eat.

Your teen knows that one of your primary jobs is to feed him and that once you had almost total control over what he ate, so to him, food can represent both parental love and authority. Rejecting your food choices can be a subtle way of asserting his independence. Neuropsychological developments in teenagers mean he also craves immediate, rewarding hits. Less nutritional foods, high in sugar and carbs, can feel intensely rewarding and lead him to reject healthier options.

WHAT YOU MIGHT BE THINKING

If there's plenty to eat, you may feel annoyed that he's dismissing the food you've provided. You might be worried, too, that he's eating food with a low nutritional value instead and so isn't getting a balanced diet.

WHAT HE MIGHT BE THINKING

⊚ **Now that he can make** more choices of his own, eating the junk food that you try to limit can be a way of rebelling against your authority.

⊚ **After being told** what to do all day at school, this comment may be a way of venting against adult authority in a safe space.

⊚ **Triggering your guilt** that you aren't providing for him may be a way to get your attention.

⊚ **He may think he can eat** what he likes, not realizing that some teenagers start to gain weight now.

⊚ **When seeking instant** gratification, he thinks about how good a food will make him feel right away, not how healthy it is.

⊚ **Peer pressure** can fuel a love of "junk" food. Sharing candy, chips, and energy drinks helps him bond with friends. By comparison, healthy food at home feels boring.

▶ SEE RELATED TOPICS ◀
Peer pressure and "FOMO": pp.58–59
I'm not hungry in the morning: pp.70–71

❝ ❞

TEENAGERS CRAVE IMMEDIATE, REWARDING HITS FROM FOOD.

HOW YOU COULD RESPOND

In the moment

Interpret his message
Rather than rushing to show him the evidence to the contrary, say you understand he can't see something to eat and that it sounds like, after a long day, he needs a snack.

Suggest alternatives
If there's nothing obvious to eat at first glance, show him how in minutes he can make a satisfying snack, such as heating soup, putting together a peanut butter sandwich, or cooking oatmeal.

In the long term

Put appetizing food at eye level
He's looking for a quick fix. Try putting fruit, juice pops, peanut butter energy balls, or hummus and carrot sticks in his eye-line when he opens the fridge, freezer, or cabinets.

Try the 80/20 rule
If around 80 percent of his diet at home is healthy (and he exercises) and 20 percent is treat-based, he's less likely to buy "junk" food and can learn to exercise impulse control by deciding to make healthy choices.

Get him cooking
Involving him in cooking helps him appreciate how preparing fresh food can be enjoyable.

Eat meals together
This encourages healthy eating and keeps you connected. Studies show that family meals have a calming effect and help teens feel included and valued. Even if he doesn't say much, he sees other family members communicate and feels an important part of the unit.

Help him stand up to hype
Research shows that adolescents are more likely to change eating habits when aware of the tactics involved in food advertising. Make the most of his emerging social awareness to talk about how the food industry targets the young.

"I'VE GOT **NOTHING TO WEAR**."

For your teenager, fashion is a way both to express her identity and make it clear which social group she belongs to. So don't be surprised if your teenager becomes upset when she feels that she can't get her "uniform" for a party quite right.

SCENARIO | Your teenager is complaining that she has nothing to wear for a party.

This period of experimentation—when teenagers are working out how they want to look—comes at a time when their concerns about fitting in make them acutely self-conscious and worried about their chosen outfit. Although not as fashion-focused as girls, many boys also use clothes, particularly designer casual wear and sneakers, to mark social status and to signal belonging to certain cliques.

But not all teens use clothes to get noticed. Less confident youngsters may use them to cover up their bodies and to avoid attracting attention.

WHAT YOU MIGHT BE THINKING

You may be annoyed that she's saying she's got nothing to wear while staring into a full closet. You may worry she seems to have a throwaway attitude to clothes, which will never be satisfied and is environmentally unsustainable.

WHAT SHE MIGHT BE THINKING

⊚ **For your teenager**, not being able to spot an outfit instantly can feel like a catastrophe. She may be eager to mirror what friends are wearing so that she feels accepted at the party and secure in her choice.

⊚ **Conflictingly**, she may want to stand out but still get noticed and admired. If she's a "style leader" in her clique, she'll also pride herself on not looking "ordinary" or the same as everyone else.

⊚ **She'll want an outfit** that photographs well for social media, where it will be seen and judged by many more peers. She may not want to wear one that's already appeared online.

⊚ **Her angry feelings** could be masking feelings of anxiety and insecurity. She may be worried she's gained weight (even though she may just have grown) and scared she won't look as good as her friends. You're an easy target for her feelings.

SEE RELATED TOPICS
How tall will I get?: pp.32–33
All my friends look amazing: pp.122–123

HOW YOU COULD RESPOND

In the moment

Acknowledge her feelings
Rather than argue, let her express her frustration. Say, "You sound worried about finding an outfit." Uncontradicted, a strong feeling can fade in just 90 seconds.

Talk about growing up
If her clothes don't fit, talk about how her body develops. Girls can put on 20 percent of their body weight in puberty, often gaining pounds before growth spurts. However, if you think she's gaining more weight than is healthy, don't bring this up now, as it will trigger more panic.

Help her be creative
Chat about the kind of look she's seeking and help her achieve this with the clothes she has. Could online styling tools give her an idea of what suits her proportions?

Ask why she feels pressure
Question why she feels she never has enough clothes. Did someone make a remark on social media, or does this come from her own feelings of inadequacy? Explain how recognizing these voices can help her reject them and ease the pressure.

In the long term

Discuss sustainable fashion
Talk about the human cost of sweatshops and fast fashion. Ten percent of the world's carbon footprint comes from the clothing industry, so clothes should never be throwaway, one-use items.

Help her take responsibility
Give her a monthly clothing budget so she learns she can't have everything she feels she needs.

Suggest swapping and sharing
Sharing clothes with siblings and friends or using a clothes exchange site can help her avoid being pictured in one outfit too often.

Help her get organized
If she's lost track of the clothes she has, suggest a sorting session. She could put on some music and spend an hour sorting clothes by type, giving any she doesn't wear or that don't fit to charity.

Deal with weight worries
If she recognizes she's gained too much weight or is underweight, find a time when she's calm and suggest she writes down body image worries to externalize these and find ways to deal with them.

SOCIAL MEDIA

Social media allows teenagers to be constantly connected to friends. However, they also need help to find a balance so that time spent on screens isn't at the expense of real-world activities.

It helps if parents remember that adolescents use social media to do the same things that we did at their age—gossip, hang out together, and flirt.

The difference is, when young people conduct their social lives on phones, there are fewer boundaries.

As the frontal cortex of your teen's brain—responsible for judgment and self-control—is still under construction, they may find it harder to manage distractions and temptations. This means that you may need to help them work out some limits around their social media use.

" "

TEENAGERS NEED GUIDANCE TO HELP THEM BALANCE SCREEN TIME WITH REAL-WORLD COMMUNICATION.

1
Make it a health issue
Talk about phone use as a health issue, like nutrition or sleep. Explain how their best friendship moments will be in the real world and how comparison and bitchiness on social media can cause unhappiness.

4
Have phone-free zones
Introduce phone-free zones around your home— for everyone. Be a good role model by limiting your own social media and phone use.

7
Mention the "golden hour"
Research shows the more time teens spend online, the more likely they are to get caught up in cyberbullying. An hour a day is seen as long enough to keep up with peers but short enough to avoid conflict.

WORKING THINGS OUT

8 key principles

2
Encourage questioning
Before posting a picture, suggest they check their motives. Is your teen trying to look popular or win approval to make them feel better? Are they mindful that peers are showcasing an edited "highlight reel" of their lives?

3
Explain how social media hooks them in
Discuss how add-ons—such as location-tracking maps, which show where friends are, and "streaks," which reward them for constantly returning to their screen—are set up by social networks to trigger "fear of missing out." Once they see how social media is designed to act on them, they're more likely to resist these ploys.

5
Discuss boundaries
They may already recognize how distracting social media can be. Work as a team. Suggest an app that sets a daily limit on their use of social media and allows you to see it, too.

6
Note how phones make us feel
They may notice how constant updates are distracting and also how rejected they feel when a friend would rather watch a screen than talk. Point out, too, how overuse has physical symptoms, such as eye strain and back pain, and can make them feel overwhelmed.

8
Introduce a digital sunset
Adolescents who overuse phones are 52 percent more likely to have less than 7 hours' sleep a night, which affects their health, well-being, and schoolwork. Make bedrooms device-free at night and have a rule of no screens for at least an hour before bedtime.

"THEY'RE **SO CUTE**."

Your child may have had her first crush in elementary school. However, the onset of puberty, which is accompanied by a dramatic increase in the hormones that govern sex drives and an urge to bond, means she may feel these attractions more intensely now.

SCENARIO | You spot a name, surrounded by love hearts, on your teen's homework diary.

Your teen's crush lets her practice being powerfully attached to someone who's not a parent and try out a more adult role. However, a real relationship would be too much for her now, so it's easier for her to desire unattainable people, such as a peer she hardly knows,

a pop star, or even a teacher. The result is often one-sided and played out in her imagination. Her feelings will fade when she learns more about her crush and stops idealizing them. In the meantime, she's learning to deal with powerful feelings of desire.

WHAT YOU MIGHT BE THINKING

You may worry that she's being obsessive and her feelings may get hurt. If her crush is on an older person, you may fret that she could be taken advantage of.

"

WITH THE ONSET OF PUBERTY, TEENAGERS CAN FEEL INTENSE ATTRACTIONS.

WHAT SHE MIGHT BE THINKING

- **At this age**, girls are thought to devote 34 percent of their strong emotions to real or imagined relationships, and boys devote 25 percent. While girls may talk about their crush, boys are more likely to be secretive for fear of being teased.

- **Your teen's crush is nerve-wracking** and exciting. She may believe she's in love and feel euphoric. She may also be unsure about managing her emotions and how to get her crush to notice her. For the first time, she's thinking about how she's viewed sexually and may feel she's falling short.

- **She's projecting** all the things she finds attractive onto an idealized version of her crush. She may think up elaborate scenarios to ask them out and may even write songs or poetry about them.

HOW YOU COULD RESPOND

In the moment

Acknowledge her feelings
Let her know it's okay to have a crush on a peer of either gender and that she can simply enjoy the experience. If you suspect she has a crush on a teacher, talk about this. Say her feelings will likely pass and she should avoid acting on them.

Talk about relationships
Use her crush as a chance to talk about loving relationships. While a crush may give you goose-bumps and make you feel nervous, love develops over time and is based on an equal relationship in which both people know each other intimately.

Avoid too many questions
Parents need to provide a supportive, predictable home life so that if her heart gets broken, she can fall back into a familiar routine.

In the long term

Discuss boundaries
Explain that however strong her feelings are, she shouldn't message her crush inappropriately or allow her attention to embarrass them.

Give her context
Point out that the object of her affection is a person with feelings and flaws, not an object to lust over because of their looks.

Help her monitor her feelings
The anticipation of getting social media updates on a crush brings an instant hit to the brain's reward circuitry. Suggest limiting check-ups to 5 minutes a day to keep a crush from impacting friendships and schoolwork.

Help her face reality
Prepare her for disappointment by explaining she may need to meet lots of people before finding a reciprocal relationship. Reassure her that if her affection isn't returned, her hurt feelings will fade.

SEE RELATED TOPICS
He shared this picture: pp.76–77
He's just a friend: pp.108–109

"IT'S ALWAYS **MY FAULT**."

Even when he knows he's done something wrong, your teenager may find it hard to accept responsibility. Framing the behavior that you'd like to change in a more constructive way will help head off denials and tone down defensive reactions.

SCENARIO | You find a wet towel on the bathroom floor after your teen has showered and ask if it's his.

There's a complex mix of reasons why your teen is sensitive about being blamed. If he already feels inadequate, criticism from an adult confirms his fears. At the same time, his growing independence means he questions your authority. Rejecting your judgment protects his ego. Or he may genuinely struggle to grasp how his habits affect others. All this sensitivity comes at a time when parents, eager to encourage responsibility, may be more critical.

However, if he feels constantly blamed, he may worry he's a disappointment and distance himself to protect against these painful feelings.

WHAT YOU MIGHT BE THINKING

If you're trying to encourage responsible behavior, it's frustrating when he throws criticism back, saying you're being unreasonable. You may worry he'll struggle in life if he doesn't take responsibility.

WHAT HE MIGHT BE THINKING

⊙ **Even if he's responsible**, he finds it easier to turn feelings of shame and resentment back onto you rather than deal with them.

⊙ **Saying "It's always my fault"** helps him paint himself as a victim of your unreasonable behavior and distracts from the underlying reason you made the comment.

⊙ **He may think** you expect him to be perfect at all times and that he can't live up to your standards, so he gives up even trying.

⊙ **If he often says,** "It's always my fault," it could signal that he feels automatically blamed. Over time, to avoid your criticism, he may close down, disconnect, or become hostile.

◤ **SEE RELATED TOPICS** ◢
Communicating with teens: pp.46–47
You always criticize: pp.148–149

" "
TEENAGERS OFTEN FIND IT HARD TO ACCEPT RESPONSIBILITY AND FEEL SENSITIVE ABOUT BEING BLAMED.

HOW YOU COULD RESPOND

In the moment

Be specific
Rather than outright accusation, use "I feel" statements. Try, "I feel frustrated when towels are left on the floor because they don't dry and become smelly."

Criticize the action, not the person, and give a reason
Be clear you're not criticizing him as a person or singling him out—you expect the whole household to act the same. Explain the towel won't dry if it's not hung up.

Don't be deterred by defensive reactions
If he says you always criticize, stay neutral. Reframe your position by stating the problem. After you've brought it up once, gently saying one word, "towel," may do the trick.

Ask him for his view and stay calm
Ask what he thinks he could have done differently. If he uses his own mental processes to work out what he did wrong, he's more likely to recall this.

In the long term

Check your language
If you tend to blame him a lot, talk to an objective family member or friend to work out why. Break the cycle by making four positive comments for each complaint.

Understand this is a stage
Studies show that between 13 and 16 years old, adolescent boys in particular show a temporary decline in their ability to recognize and respond to feelings of annoyance. He may not realize how irritating some of his behavior is.

Be a good role model
If you make an error in judgment, admit this to teach him how to take responsibility.

Tell him perfection isn't possible
Say no one is perfect so he knows you don't expect him to be—and so he realizes that he's not a disappointment when he gets things wrong.

"I HATE YOU!"

Teenagers have intense emotions, and the way in which they express them can be extreme. They also want independence and control over their lives. If your teen feels you're in her way, she may interpret overpowering frustration as hatred.

SCENARIO | Your teen screams that she hates you when you take away her phone so she doesn't stay up late messaging friends.

Clashes are common between teens and parents. Teenagers get angry when they feel that adults don't understand or respect them, while parents can get annoyed if they feel they're losing control.

If your teenager feels you're stopping her communicating with her friends she'll be especially annoyed. Her connection with them may feel more important than your approval. Afraid of missing out, this will have triggered the primal fight-or-flight regions of her lower brain at the expense of logical, rational thought processes.

WHAT YOU MIGHT BE THINKING

When you've spent years loving and raising your child, it can be a shock to hear her say something so hurtful. You might wonder if you've done something wrong as a parent to prompt this outburst.

WHAT SHE MIGHT BE THINKING

◉ **Like many of her generation**, your teenager was probably encouraged during childhood to be more honest about her emotions—both love and hate—than perhaps you were. So these words may not feel quite as serious to her.

◉ **Your teen is very angry**. Young people feel having a phone is a basic human right, like being fed and clothed, and she's lashing out because she doesn't yet understand the need for limits.

◉ **These words are her last resort** to show you how much she wants to get her way. If she's in the middle of a friendship drama, removing her phone may feel like a life and death matter.

◉ **Underneath, teens know** they're not supposed to say such cruel things to their parents, who've invested so much love in them. After an outburst, she's likely to feel guilty, even though she may still struggle to apologize, unless you talk through what happened.

HOW YOU COULD RESPOND

In the moment

Don't take it personally
Reminding yourself that she's reacting against your boundaries, not you, will help you stay calm.

Show you're listening
She's in an aroused emotional state. Name her feelings in short, clear sentences so she knows you understand. Say, "I can see you're angry that you're not allowed to have your phone."

Understand what lies beneath
Realize she's trying to shock you into giving in by saying the most extreme thing she can think of.

Defuse the situation
Your first instinct may be to demand an apology, but this will enrage her more in her aroused state. Say, "We'll talk when we're calmer" so she has time to revert to using her logical, higher brain.

In the long term

Prioritize sleep
Many teens struggle to regulate emotions because they're sleep deprived. A third get less than 7 hours a night. A lack of sleep affects the complex emotional centers of the brain, making teens more likely to lash out.

Suggest alternative reactions
When she's calmer, explain that insults never help. Praise her next time when she deals with strong feelings in a more measured way.

Help her learn empathy
Talk about how it felt to hear those words. Explain that however angry she is, she should treat others with dignity and respect.

Be consistent
If you tend to give in to demands to protect her from disappointment or to avoid fights, she may lash out more if she doesn't get her way. Maintain clear boundaries.

SEE RELATED TOPICS
I didn't slam the door!: pp.80–81
It's my phone: pp.96–97

❝ ❞

EXTREME EMOTIONS CAN MAKE ISSUES SEEM BLACK AND WHITE TO TEENAGERS.

COMMUNICATING
WITH TEENS

Teenagers' brains are still developing the functions that help them control primal fight-or-flight instincts. As a result, they tend to shout more, be moodier, and be more sensitive.

Teenagers' extreme reactions can hamper communication because they make it harder for parents to give teens what they really want from them—love and understanding.

Your teenager may talk to you less now and be more prickly to deal with, but it's helpful to recognize that they're behaving in this way because they're learning to deal with complicated emotions—as well as asserting their independence.

Even if the flow of conversation you once enjoyed has slowed to a trickle, it's critical to keep communication open. They still need to know that you're there for them when they're not quite ready to go it alone.

> " "
>
> IT'S HELPFUL TO RECOGNIZE THAT TEENAGERS ARE LEARNING TO DEAL WITH COMPLICATED EMOTIONS.

1
Pick your moment
Look for signs your teen wants to talk, such as hanging around, dropping hints about issues at school, or asking for help to find things at bedtime.

4
Validate feelings
Teens appreciate it if you try to understand how they feel. Even if it's hard, accept their feelings. Describe them, too. Try, "I'm sorry you feel angry/sad."

6
Avoid quick fixes
Rushing to fix problems can make your teen feel their worries are trivial and you want their problems to go away.

8
Use "I" statements
Rather than say, "You were wrong," say, "I feel that …." They're likely to feel closer to you if you express feelings.

WORKING THINGS OUT

10 key principles

2
Set aside time
Spend regular, unhurried time together, just doing things they like to do. These "emotional deposits" remind them that you like, as well as love, them.

3
Listen more than you talk
Responding with just a nod or "I see" is often all that's needed. What you don't say rather than what you do can make you the best sounding board.

5
Check your facial expressions
Research shows that teens tend to interpret facial expressions more negatively. Try to adopt a happy, relaxed expression when you talk to them, or they may think you're being critical.

7
Watch your tone
Shouting triggers teens' already sensitive fight-or-flight responses, making them more reactive. Avoid name-calling, too. Hearing insults from the most important people in their lives can embed them in your teen's self-image. Be clear that it's their behavior you disapprove of, not them.

9
Avoid lecturing
Giving advice makes teens defensive. If you feel your teen is holding back, try, "Do you think I'll react badly if…?" Thank them for sharing so they see you'll comfort rather than judge them.

10
Don't take it personally
Parents may feel rejected by teens' monosyllabic replies and withdraw, too. Remind yourself that separating from you is healthy and that they still love and appreciate you.

TAILORED ADVICE

Age by age

13–14 YEAR-OLDS

Help them find the words
Young teens may not have the vocabulary to express themselves. Use "feeling" words so they pick these up, and summarize what they're trying to say.

Listen to complaints
Your teen contains their behavior all day at school, so don't feel you need to do anything but listen when they complain. Say, "Do you want my help, or do you just want to unload?"

15–16 YEAR-OLDS

Reframe questions
Try humor. Ask, "What made you laugh today?" or "If today was an emotion, what would it be?"

Find new opportunities
Offer to take your busy teen to and from places so you can chat in the car.

17–18 YEAR-OLDS

Make decisions together
Brainstorm solutions about your teen's future. Talk to them respectfully, not as though they're still a child.

Use tech
If they've left home, send a nice text or a funny GIF to remind your teen you love and think about them.

"I SHOWERED LAST WEEK."

As a child, your teenager was used to you telling him when to wash. Now that his body is changing, he may not yet recognize that some of those physical changes affect the way he smells, as well as the way he looks.

SCENARIO | You've noticed your teen is smelly, but he resists showering regularly.

In adolescence, the body's 2 to 4 million sweat glands, including the apocrine glands—found mainly in the armpits—become more active. Apocrine gland fluid is odorless, but when bacteria decompose it, it releases a strong smell, which can be pungent enough to fill your teen's room. This sweat doesn't cool his body; it's released in response to excitement and stress, which he is more prone to. He can also release temperature-regulating sweat during exercise, so ideally he should wash every day.

WHAT YOU MIGHT BE THINKING

You may worry his peers will laugh at him behind his back and be concerned that he isn't learning to take care of himself. You may be unsure about how to approach the topic without hurting his feelings or sounding critical.

WHAT HE MIGHT BE THINKING

⊚ **He may not realize** he has body odor. Studies show that because this is a new smell to teenagers, they don't immediately identify it as their own sweat. Or, if he's had body odor for a while, he may be so used to it that he's stopped noticing it.

⊚ **He may feel that showering** gets in the way of other things he'd rather be doing.

⊚ **If he's unaware** of his odor, he may hear your comments as criticism—especially if friends haven't pointed it out.

⊚ **To him, your comments** can sound nagging and controlling. He may be resisting washing to show that he's in charge of his body and will decide how to take care of it. If you ask him repeatedly to wash, he may tune you out.

◀ **SEE RELATED TOPICS** ▶
I've got too much to do: pp.52–53
You always criticize: pp.148–149

> **"** **"**
>
> AS HIS BODY
> CHANGES, A DAILY
> SHOWER IS
> ADVISABLE.

HOW YOU COULD RESPOND

In the moment

Talk directly
Say in a warm, matter-of-fact way, "I love you, and it smells as though you're a bit sweaty. It's just your body doing its job and a sign that you need a shower."

Point out how quick showering is
If he thinks he's too busy, tell him that 5 minutes can be all it takes to have a thorough wash with some soap.

Help him consider what others think
While teens aren't good at smelling their own sweat, he may have noticed other people's. Talk to him about how people view body odor and explain that self-care sends out a message that he likes and respects himself.

Keep reminders brief
If he needs another prompt, gently saying one word, "Shower?", may be enough, because he already knows the reasons.

In the long term

Make it enjoyable and easy
Give him a choice of soaps, gels, and deodorants. Talk about how a shower can be a relaxing, private way to unwind. Put a laundry basket in his room, too, to remind him that he needs to wear fresh clothes daily.

Compliment his cleanliness
Always pointing out he needs a shower will make him defensive. Say how fresh he smells when you notice. The compliment will reinforce the positives of showering.

Check for other reasons
If the problem continues, it could be because he doesn't see washing as a priority, he doesn't understand how others view him, or it's an act of defiance. Continue to support him so he doesn't face social disapproval. If he's recently dropped a hygiene routine and neglects his appearance, he may be suffering from low self-esteem or depression. Check if his social life and schoolwork are also suffering.

"SHE'S SUCH A **BITCH!**"

When it comes to teenage friendships, parents tend to worry about bullying. However, more common and just as upsetting are the day-to-day fallouts within groups of friends, known as "relational aggression."

SCENARIO | When you ask your teen why she hasn't invited her best friend to her party, she says they've fallen out because "she's such a bitch."

Even within close-knit groups of teenage friends, there are fallouts. Within groups, members unconsciously fall into a hierarchy, often with a "queen bee" figure at the top. Conflict can flare up when unwritten rules are broken or friends find themselves in competition. Members may flex their social status by excluding others, and a decision may be made that a member "deserves" to be ostracized. Relational aggression is hard to spot, but the isolation and stress it causes has been found to be as painful as physical blows.

WHAT YOU MIGHT BE THINKING

You may be confused, as this is the first time she's mentioned she and her friend aren't talking. You may be baffled, as just recently they seemed close, and also wonder where the anger and strong language have come from.

WHAT SHE MIGHT BE THINKING

◉ **Teens are proud** to be in charge of their social lives, so she may be embarrassed to admit that she's had a major fallout.

◉ **If she's guilty** of mean behavior and of trying to teach her friend a lesson by not inviting her to the party, she's likely to have a list of reasons her friend deserves to be left off the guest list to justify her actions.

◉ **She may have been worried** about telling you because she knows she's said and done things that don't reflect well on her. She may also be worried that you'll get involved and talk to the school or the other girl's parents.

◉ **If the fight has spilled** out onto social media, she may be anxious about checking her phone, as she'll want to monitor comments. She may be tempted to make herself feel better by posting comments or untagging her friend from pictures.

HOW YOU COULD RESPOND

In the moment

Listen first
Admitting a falling-out can be hard. Listen to her reasons for excluding her friend without judging. Bear in mind, though, that you're getting just one side of the story.

See it in context
Reassure yourself that power plays happen inside all friend groups—and that teens need to learn how to handle normal social conflict.

Suggest she is kinder
Is she excluding her former best friend because she now finds her annoying, too clingy, or she's moved on? Or is she not inviting her in revenge for a slight? If she's doing the cutting off, talk about how it's always possible to dial down a friendship rather than sever it abruptly with no explanation.

Help her assess her actions
At a neutral time, ask her to look back on what happened. If she ever catches herself thinking that her former friend "deserved" her treatment, ask her to question her justifications.

In the long term

Give her resolution scripts
Teens can end up ignoring friends because they don't have the words to resolve rifts. Explain that apologies show strength and suggest nonconfrontational ways to address rifts such as, "Our friendship is important to me. Can we talk about what's wrong?"

Set a good example
Show how you consider others. Make it a family value that everyone deserves to be treated with dignity and respect.

Encourage her to open up
Some teens may feel that talking about friendship issues is a weakness. If she holds back, help her to express social worries.

SEE RELATED TOPICS
Peer pressure and "FOMO": pp.58–59
Friendship issues: pp.64–65

❝ ❞

DAY-TO-DAY FALLOUTS CAN CAUSE PAINFUL FEELINGS OF ISOLATION AND STRESS.

"I'VE GOT **TOO MUCH** TO DO."

Once, when teens finished their school day, most of their work was done. Now, this is often the start of a second shift of extracurricular activities, homework, and test preparation. The result is that your teen can feel overwhelmed unless you help her manage her time.

SCENARIO | Home late after orchestra practice, your teen looks stressed and says she doesn't have time to complete her homework and study for a test.

Today's teens are tested almost constantly, and standardized tests are increasingly difficult. With a more competitive work market, too, teens feel they should maximize each moment with extracurricular activities to stand out. Furthermore, sports that were once simply fun get more competitive. Research shows that teens often spend any downtime left on social media, even though the more time spent there, the more socially insecure they can feel, compounding their stress.

WHAT YOU MIGHT BE THINKING

You may think she has to work hard now so that she has more choices when she leaves school. If she says she can't cope, you may feel powerless to help, both emotionally and practically.

WHAT SHE MIGHT BE THINKING

◉ **At this age**, adolescents are prone to "all or nothing" thinking. If she can't see how she'll complete all of her homework, as well as prepare for her test, she'll feel trapped and hopeless and may also be scared of getting into trouble at school.

◉ **To try to keep up**, she may sacrifice sleep, which makes her more emotional and tired and less able to juggle everything.

◉ **Girls in particular** can be overly conscientious, feeling that they need to do everything perfectly, which becomes harder as schoolwork gets more demanding.

◉ **She may have** so many tasks to complete, she doesn't know where to start. If she's overwhelmed, she's more likely to project these feelings onto you as a way of managing them.

SEE RELATED TOPICS
I am studying: pp.128–129
Test support: pp.134–135

HOW YOU COULD RESPOND

In the moment

Talk it through
Thank her for telling you, as it's not easy for a conscientious teen to ask for help. Reduce the intensity of her emotion by staying calm to signal that the situation isn't as serious as she fears. Listen while she tells you what she still has to do tonight.

Give practical suggestions
To help her prioritize tasks and break work down into manageable chunks, suggest listing jobs under important, vital, and critical, then see what's achievable.

Help her avoid procrastination
Suggest she spends only 5 minutes on her hardest task first. Once she overcomes her fear of starting, she's likely to keep going.

Put it in perspective
Girls especially can measure worth by grades. Say that not every piece of work has to be perfect and that perfectionism can affect well-being.

In the long term

Take the pressure off
Avoid attaching goals to extracurricular activities. Let her choose which ones she sticks with based on what she enjoys.

Help her recognize stress
Suggest she keeps a mental sliding scale: 1 means "I feel good" and 10 "I feel burned out." If it gets to 8, it's time to try to reduce stress levels.

Manage your stress
Parental stress is contagious, so model self-care. Whether you take a bath, work out, or read a book, model wind-down strategies.

Enjoy goal-free time
Prioritize family meals and activities where the aim is just to enjoy time together. Rather than organize activities each weekend, encourage unstructured downtime.

Discuss her schedule
Set aside time to talk about how to balance commitments. When she has time off, suggest she limits time on social media and talks to friends instead.

" "

TEENS CAN FEEL OVERWHELMED BY COMPETING DEMANDS AND NEED YOUR HELP TO COPE.

"I SKIPPED LUNCH."

The school cafeteria may just look like a room to eat in to adults, but for teenagers, it can feel like an extremely challenging environment. Teens feel enormous pressure to fit in, and some would rather miss lunch and go hungry than risk having to sit on their own in full view of their peers.

SCENARIO | When you ask your teenager why he's starving when he gets home, he says that he skipped lunch because he had no one to sit with.

There can be many reasons why your teenager had no one to sit with at lunch. An extra lesson may have meant that his usual group weren't in the cafeteria at the same time and he didn't want to eat alone. Or he may have been excluded if he has fallen out with a more socially powerful member. Not joining others may also have been his choice.

Perhaps he's not interested in joining the hierarchy of students in his grade year and is a "floater" who prefers to be independent. Or he may be being left out if he has less-developed social skills and struggles to understand how his behavior is viewed by others. This may make other teens uncomfortable, so he may be excluded as a result.

WHAT YOU MIGHT BE THINKING

Hearing your son say he's skipping lunch because he has no friends may bring back difficult memories if this ever happened to you at school. You may also worry that he won't be able to concentrate if he's hungry.

SEE RELATED TOPICS
Friendship issues: pp.64–65
I'm staying in: pp.132–133

WHAT HE MIGHT BE THINKING

⊙ **If your son is struggling** to make friends, he may feel "weird" and believe that he's unpopular. He may worry this is a label that will stick in the school hierarchy.

⊙ **If he has social anxiety,** he may feel invisible to peers, yet also as if he stands out for not fitting in.

⊙ **Your son may try to deal** with painful feelings of rejection by projecting them outward. He may say he doesn't like anyone at school or that they are all stupid or below him.

⊙ **Teens are desperate** to find a new group as they move away from their families, so he's likely to be ashamed and embarrassed to tell you that he has yet to find a new group to accept him.

❝ ❞

FOR TEENAGERS, THE SCHOOL CAFETERIA CAN LOOK LIKE A TERRIFYING PLACE TO NAVIGATE.

HOW YOU COULD RESPOND

In the moment

Find out why
Was this a one-off, or has he missed lunch a lot to avoid being seen eating alone? Has he fallen out with friends? Or does he always find it hard to form friendships?

Empathize
Resist telling him to work harder at making friends. He could feel like it's his fault and withdraw more. Appreciate how embarrassing it was for him to admit this.

Brainstorm alternatives
Can he eat a packed lunch elsewhere in the school? Or sign up to a lunchtime club where interests are shared and go to lunch with them afterward? Does he know how to ask a group if he can sit with them?

Give him perspective
Talk about how everyone goes through times when they feel left out and that he can work through these feelings.

In the long term

Share strategies if he's socially anxious
If he feels there's a spotlight on him, help him imagine turning it onto others. Suggest turning his focus outward by looking for details such as what others are eating.

Talk about developing social skills
Discuss how he can work on social skills, such as listening carefully and responding appropriately.

Be a friend at home
If he feels rejected, he may be suffering from low self-worth. Make it clear you enjoy spending time in his company.

Help him widen his social circle
Discuss how schools foster rigid social hierarchies that don't exist in the real world. Remind him that he'll have far more of a choice of friends when he leaves. Suggest activities outside school, such as volunteering, where he's judged on character and enthusiasm, not social skills.

"THAT'S **KIDS' STUFF**."

You may have spent time and money on extracurricular lessons for your child. You may also have thought these will be useful on future application forms. So it can be a shock if your teen says she no longer wants to carry on with an activity.

SCENARIO | After years of piano lessons, your teen says she wants to give up.

As your teen's independence grows, she wants control over her time, especially if she has other priorities now, such as hanging out with friends. She may also start to compare her achievements to those of peers and may be put off an activity if others are getting further ahead in it. Or she may be rejecting a hobby that she views as part of her childhood so that she can feel more grown-up now.

WHAT YOU MIGHT BE THINKING

You may think your investment will go to waste before she gets to a level to impress employers or universities. You may worry she lacks staying power. But if lessons have become a battleground, secretly, you may feel relief.

SEE RELATED TOPICS
I've got too much to do: pp.52–53
Peer pressure and FOMO: pp.58–59

" "
AS INDEPENDENCE GROWS, TEENS WANT TO MANAGE THEIR TIME.

WHAT SHE MIGHT BE THINKING

◉ **If your teen has learned** an instrument from a young age, this may account for half of her life. She may feel it's time to focus on other things she's more interested in.

◉ **A key reason** teens give up activities is because parents become overly invested. If she feels pressure to perform, then she may prefer to give up now rather than endure the stress or risk not meeting your expectations.

◉ **As the level of achievement** increases, she may be unwilling to give the required commitment of time and effort, especially now that she has more schoolwork. Also, if others are starting to excel where she isn't, she may want to avoid feeling inferior.

◉ **If friends are giving up** activities, she may not want to feel like she's missing out on meet-ups. She may want more free time rather than spending even more time after school being told what to do.

HOW YOU COULD RESPOND

In the moment

Ask about the underlying reasons
Listen, then summarize back to her so she knows you've understood. Are her reasons temporary, or has a genuine dislike built up?

Discuss the upsides
Chat about how playing an instrument has many benefits, from being relaxing to aiding memory, while a love of sports will help keep her healthy for life.

Ask her to honor commitments
If you agree she can drop her activity, suggest she waits until the end of the term to teach her about the importance of honoring commitments. Rather than worry about lack of staying power, see it as her learning to admit when she has too much on her plate. She'll also appreciate that you respected her choice.

In the long term

Help her gain perspective
Many grown-ups regret giving up activities when younger and often return to them. Even older teens become nostalgic about pastimes they gave up. Suggest she talks to other young people who either gave up an activity or persevered to help her weigh the pros and cons. If she still wants to stop, respect her choice and the fact that she's considered it carefully.

Explore other activities
Your teen needs to feel that she's good at certain activities, otherwise she may become dependent on peers for approval. The brain is still developing until the mid-twenties, so if she's determined to give up this activity, there's still time for her to develop a new skill easily that makes her feel confident.

PEER **PRESSURE** AND **"FOMO"**

Parents tend to see peer pressure and FOMO— fear of missing out—as hidden forces, mysteriously taking over teens and encouraging risky behavior.

As teens start to move away from family, being accepted by a new group—their friends—feels critical. Experiencing peer pressure is partly about belonging to this new group. At 13–14 years old, when risky behavior peaks, teens may go along with the crowd rather than feel left out.

Research shows that just being in the presence of friends can make teens behave more irresponsibly. Teens also suffer more anxiety than adults when excluded. This need to belong makes them more vulnerable to the fear of missing out (FOMO) on what peers are doing.

1
Get perspective
If friends are responsible, hard-working, and supportive, you'll welcome peer pressure. Bear in mind, too, that we never grow out of feeling peer pressure, but teens are more susceptible to it.

4
Beware of dares
Suggest that when friends plan something risky or irresponsible or suggest a dare, it can be just as funny—and less risky— to imagine it as to do it.

6
Play "What if?"
Pose friendly questions such as, "What if you're dared to play a drinking game?" Let them ask questions, too, so it works both ways and they hear how you'd handle a difficult situation.

WORKING THINGS OUT

8 key principles

2

Highlight negative peer pressure
Your teen may not recognize peer pressure at work. Suggest they ask themselves questions such as, "What am I being asked to do?", "Why do I feel uncomfortable?", or "Why do I feel that this isn't right?"

3

Talk about FOMO
Mention how being able to see what friends are up to all the time on social media is linked to negative feelings such as stress. Suggest they self-regulate their use. If they do find they've been left out, help them focus on their own positive activities, whether it's a relaxing night in or a family BBQ.

5

Discuss how the brain works
The part of the brain that puts the brakes on risky behavior—the prefrontal cortex—isn't fully developed until the mid-twenties. This knowledge can help your teen recognize there will be situations they're not mature enough to handle, and remind them they need more time to make decisions.

7

Help her practice saying "No"
It's hard to say "No" in the moment. Suggest scripts they can use such as, "This isn't my kind of thing", "I'm not comfortable with that", or even just a clear "No, thanks."

8

Be a good role model
Talk about decisions you've made, both good and bad, and how some were affected by you wanting to conform while other times you stood up to peers. In daily life, show how you stand up to others to do what's right, even when it's difficult or inconvenient.

TAILORED ADVICE

Age by age

13–14
YEAR-OLDS

Offer a get-out clause
The wish to conform peaks now. Suggest they use you as an excuse, saying, "My parents would kill me!"

Provide a meeting place
Invite their friends into your home to get to know them and provide a safe space.

15–16
YEAR-OLDS

Keep talking
Chat about what your teen does with friends to give you an idea of their developing values.

Recruit caring young adults
Studies show that teens are more likely to take advice on alcohol, drugs, and sex from a peer such as an older sibling or cousin rather than a parent.

17–18
YEAR-OLDS

Discuss strategies
If your teen is leaving home for college, discuss how to avoid feeling pressured to, for example, binge-drink, stay out late, or take drugs.

Talk about driving
Young people are more likely to crash when carrying a passenger, possibly due to driving faster to look cool. Discuss how peer pressure can affect safety.

"I NEED A NEW BRA."

To a teenage girl, her breasts are the most visible sign—to herself and others—that she's becoming sexually mature. She associates them with sex and, eventually, motherhood, so she may feel uncomfortable talking to you about their changing size.

SCENARIO | Your teen complains that her bras don't fit comfortably or look good under her clothes.

One of the physical changes your daughter may worry about most will be her breasts, which stop growing about 2 years after her first period.

In early adolescence, desperate to hide her growing sexuality from you, she may be shy about acknowledging them. However, as she gets used to these changes, she may feel more comfortable asking for your help to find bras. Finding a good fit so her breasts don't feel "in the way" will help her feel positive about her developing body.

WHAT YOU MIGHT BE THINKING

You may find it hard to get used to seeing your daughter develop. You may worry about how to respond if she says negative things about her breasts, such as they're too big, too small, or a shape she doesn't like.

WHAT SHE MIGHT BE THINKING

◉ **Some girls enjoy feeling** more womanly, but some can feel uncomfortable with the attention, comments, or lingering looks they attract. She may dislike being looked at like an object or annoyed that others take sexual gratification from looking at her body.

◉ **If she's getting used to** larger breasts, she may feel self-conscious and try to cover them up—crossing her arms or wearing baggy clothes—until she learns to carry herself confidently.

◉ **If she has smaller breasts**, she may worry that they'll never develop and that she won't ever be sexually attractive.

◉ **Many girls develop** breasts asymmetrically. If she thinks hers are growing at different rates, she may feel she looks odd and worry about bra shopping.

HOW YOU COULD RESPOND

In the moment

Take a neutral approach
Thank her for asking you to help.
Ask what type of bra she wants.
Avoid commenting on her breast
size or comparing her to others,
as she'll feel self-conscious.

Suggest a sports bra
Eighty percent of 14-year-old girls
say their breasts feel uncomfortable
during sports, either bouncing or
hurting when they run. To help her
stay fit, suggest a good sports bra.

Get her professionally measured
A professional fitter may help put
her at ease. While she's growing,
try to get her measured each time
you shop for bras. Follow her cues
as to how much privacy she wants
in changing rooms.

Show her how to maintain bras
Many bras lose support if machine-
washed vigorously or if the straps
aren't tightened. A well-fitted bra
should be comfortable. Red marks
or loose straps mean it's time to
adjust or change it.

In the long term

Help her welcome her breasts
Say breasts are a beautiful part of
her body and, if she wishes, will
enable her to breastfeed. Talk
positively, too, about your breasts.
How mothers see their bodies has
a profound effect on daughters.

Talk about different looks
Chat about how breasts come in
all shapes and sizes and how they
can change over a lifetime, so she
should get regularly measured
and check for cysts and lumps.

Show affection
Dads in particular may feel less
comfortable cuddling daughters
as they develop, and girls can see
this as a rejection. Keep showing
physical affection, even if it's just
a squeeze of the hand.

Talk about posture
Girls who are shy about bigger
breasts may hunch over and
try to hide them. Tell her to
be aware of this tendency
and to stand tall, as that's
the easiest way to look
happy and confident.

> " "
> ## TO GIRLS, BREASTS ARE PART OF BEING SEXUAL BEINGS. AT FIRST, SHE MIGHT BE SHY ABOUT THEM.

SEE RELATED TOPICS
I've got nothing to wear: pp.36–37
Can I skip PE?: pp.68–69

"HE KEEPS **PICKING ON ME**."

Boys' relationships are often governed by a set of unwritten rules that define what it means to be male, which include being sporty, strong, dominant, funny, and masculine. In battles for social status, some boys can get teased for not displaying these characteristics.

SCENARIO | When you ask why your teen sees less of a friend, he says his friend has been teasing him about missing goals in recent soccer matches.

We tend to think that it's mainly girls who engage in "mean" behavior. But research has found that boys are just as likely to belittle and demean—often in the form of verbal name-calling.

However, among boys, social cruelty can be harder to recognize. For them, teasing—or banter—is the glue that bonds friendships. A clever put-down is considered an art form, signaling enviable humor. If insulted, a boy's challenge is never to look upset and, ideally, to top it with a withering comeback, showing he can take the criticism.

However, when teasing is all one way and crosses the line from humorous to humiliating, it's time for your teen to try to put a stop to it.

WHAT YOU MIGHT BE THINKING

You may feel protective of your son and worried that the situation could turn into bullying, especially if others join in. Part of you may feel that he should learn to stick up for himself a bit more.

WHAT HE MIGHT BE THINKING

◉ **Boys are often socialized** to believe that they shouldn't show weakness, so he may be ashamed to admit that another boy's teasing is upsetting him.

◉ **He might agree** that he's terrible at soccer. His self-worth could be plummeting, and at the same time his anger might be building.

◉ **As sport is a public display** and a status builder, he's likely to feel ridiculed by a boy saying he's bad at it and also humiliated that he's letting the team down.

◉ **If there's a lot of banter** in his group, he might be unsure about whether he's being picked on or not and be terrified he'll be considered a wimp if he complains in any way.

◉ **Above all**, he wants the situation to stop. He may be wary of telling you for fear you'll wade in and call up the school or a parent, which he thinks will make things worse.

▶ **SEE RELATED TOPICS** ◀
Friendship issues: pp.64–65
I'm not going to school: pp.82–83

HOW YOU COULD RESPOND

In the moment

Acknowledge his feelings
Boys can find it hard to open up about friendship issues to adults, so don't dismiss his upset. Tell him the teasing isn't his fault and he shouldn't feel ashamed.

Listen without judgment
Thank him for telling you, then listen calmly. If he cries, allow him to do so without making him feel self-conscious. Listen more than you speak, help him name how he feels, and say you're sorry that this is happening.

Don't threaten to get involved
Avoid going off the deep end in his defense, especially as you've only heard one side of the story. He needs you as a firm anchor now, not his lawyer or bodyguard.

Beware of suggesting easy fixes
Resist telling him to ignore the teasing or laugh it off. As you're not him or his age, you won't understand the complexities of the situation, and he may close down again, thinking you don't know what you're talking about.

In the long term

Help him understand teasing
Explain how the teaser may be trying to make himself look more masculine or showing off to rise up the social pecking order.

Encourage self-questioning
Questions such as "What would I say if I wasn't afraid?" and "How is this teasing holding me back in sports?" can prompt him to act.

Suggest he devises a plan
The teaser believes your son won't stand up to him. Talk about changing this perception. Bullying experts say one approach that works with boys is asking to speak to the perpetrator alone to ask for the teasing to stop. If they're in the same group, he's likely to back off rather than create drama. Your son will win respect by setting boundaries.

Spot bullying
"Normal" cruelty crosses into bullying if he's the target of ongoing, intentional intimidation. In this case, he needs your help to confront the person, being clear he wants it to stop and calling it bullying, which his peer knows has big repercussions. Suggest he record incidents and talk to his teacher about stopping it.

FRIENDSHIP ISSUES

As teenagers' independence grows, they need the acceptance of peers more than ever. You may feel your teen cares more about friends than family, but try to see their needs as a survival instinct.

Humans are pack animals who rely on each other for protection. As teens prepare to leave the protection of their families, they've always needed to find another group. A sense of belonging is crucial—once, isolation would have meant certain death. There's also a physical reason why teens seem to care about friends above all else. Scans have found the reward centers in their brains are triggered more often by interactions with peers.

At the same time, they're learning to manage their emotions and impulses, as well as seeking a place in the social hierarchy. Social conflict is inevitable, but you can help your teen feel less rejected when things go wrong.

> ## THE ACCEPTANCE OF PEERS IS ALL-IMPORTANT TO TEENAGERS.

1
Say to expect conflict
Whenever groups form, there's conflict as friends try to sort out the social hierarchy. Expecting "normal" social conflict in friendships reduces feelings of hurt.

4
Suggest they pick battles
If your teen accepts they can't change other people, they can only change themselves, they're more likely to save themselves from emotionally draining fights.

6
Encourage a break
Social media means that relationship dramas can be relentless. Help them recognize when they're overwhelmed and need to switch off from their phone.

WORKING THINGS OUT

8 key principles

2
Explain types of popularity
Most teens aspire to be popular, thinking it offers protection, but popularity isn't always desirable. Research shows that 30 percent of teens are popular because they're likable, but 70 percent have status because others are afraid to cross them.

3
Emphasize quality over quantity
Teens may want lots of friends so they feel popular. However, it can take no more than two or three genuinely close friends to be happy at school. Explain it's not a numbers game.

5
See others' perspective
Known as "theory of mind," seeing another's point of view is key for friendship, fostering compromise, empathy, and listening skills. Model thinking about others' feelings. Try, "How is Jasmine now that her Dad has moved?" or "How do you think Jack feels about not being invited?"

7
Talk about a "growth" mindset
Explain that friendship is about taste and timing. If they worry they don't have enough good friends, say this doesn't mean it will always be that way. Tell them that pain from fallouts passes and encourage extracurricular activities where they'll meet others.

8
Discuss group dynamics
For cliques of girls, there's usually a "queen bee," her sidekick, and someone desperate to join. For boys, there may be a ringleader, a second-in-command, an intimidator, and a joker. Drawing a friendship tree illuminates these roles.

TAILORED ADVICE

Age by age

13–14
YEAR-OLDS

Discuss impulse control
Most friendship mistakes happen now as teens learn to contain impulses. If they want to "get back" at a peer, suggest holding back.

Be ready for fallouts
Cliques peak now, then fade as teens feel more secure. Tell them to expect power plays.

15–16
YEAR-OLDS

Advise discretion
As teens consider dating, talk about how friends may compete. Advise caution in who they open up to with intimate information.

Touch base with parents
You may not know their friends' parents. Set up a social media group to stay in the loop.

17–18
YEAR-OLDS

Encourage loyalty
Teens may start to swap old friendships for romantic ones. Encourage them not to let loyal friends down.

Discuss relationships
Help them look for the qualities in a partner that they would in a friend—someone who lifts them up and gives them the freedom to spend time with others.

"EVERYONE GETS BETTER GRADES THAN ME."

It's painful for a parent to hear their teen say they're struggling at school. If his academic confidence is falling, help your teen identify and counter negative thoughts and explain that, with work, he can improve his grades.

SCENARIO | When you ask, your teen tells you he got 52 percent on his math test.

When asked to rank themselves in elementary school, children tend to rate their abilities highly. When they are in middle school, they begin to compare themselves to others and get a clearer view of how they rank. If your teen gets negative feedback, his confidence can decline; in a competitive school environment with more rigorous standards, "average" is seen as not good enough.

WHAT YOU MIGHT BE THINKING

You first instinct may be to try to tell him that he's smart. You may also be tempted to tell him to work harder or to do his best.

WHAT HE MIGHT BE THINKING

◉ **If he's often put** in lower levels, patronized by peers showing off about higher grades, or shamed by teachers, he may believe he's not intelligent and feel there's nothing he can do about it.

◉ **If you say he's smart**, he's likely to think you're only saying this because you're his parent. Telling him to do his best may dishearten him if he's already tried and failed many times.

◉ **The transition to middle school** can be hard. If he hasn't adjusted, he may think it's his fault. He may worry about your expectations. If you did well, he may feel like he falls short and stop trying.

◉ **If he's very demoralized**, he may disengage—doing the bare minimum and even skipping class. This can turn into a vicious cycle of disengagement and anxiety.

◀ **SEE RELATED TOPICS** ▶
I've got too much to do: pp.52–53
Test support: pp.134–135

PARENTS CAN HELP TEENAGERS COUNTER NEGATIVE THOUGHTS.

HOW YOU COULD RESPOND

In the moment

Find out why he's saying it
Is it a throw-away line—a way to protect himself from failure or to lower your expectations—or is it really how he feels? Ask calm, open-ended questions.

Acknowledge that school is difficult
He may feel like it's just him struggling and that you'll dismiss his concerns. Acknowledge that school is now harder, testing at a high level, and that no one can achieve it all.

Praise effort more than grades
Don't ask how classmates did. Say the only person to beat is himself; with perseverance, he'll get better. Explain how strategies that suit his learning style can help.

Shrink the problem down to size
Home in on specific gaps in his understanding. It's normal to find some areas of a subject harder.

In the long term

Check negative thoughts
Suggest he replaces negative inner voices with the voice of a career or sports coach. Explain that the brain is like a muscle: the more it's used, the more connections are made between its network of cells and the stronger it gets. Studies show that 30 percent of teens increased IQ scores by learning new information and skills.

Explain there are many ways to be smart
If he's demoralized, tell him it's now recognized that intelligence comes in many forms. For example, it can be musical, visual, verbal and linguistic, or manual. Point out that only a few types are evaluated in tests.

Address math anxiety
Studies show that math is the subject most likely to trigger worry that can affect learning. When confronted by a math problem, some children have a flight–fight–freeze response that stops logical thinking. Help him identify this anxiety.

"CAN I **SKIP PE?**"

While they may have been happy to take part in physical education when younger, by middle school, some teenagers dread PE lessons for a variety of reasons, ranging from not feeling "sporty" enough to becoming self-conscious about their changing bodies.

SCENARIO | Your teen wants you to write a note to excuse her from physical education that day for health reasons.

It's recommended that teenagers get at least 1 hour of moderate to vigorous exercise daily. School PE lessons can help fulfill this recommendation, but many teens come to dread them, with girls tending to dislike school sports more than boys because they feel judged. At a time when teens are acutely sensitive to others' opinions, they may fear social humiliation if they don't have a partner for an activity, are picked last for a team, or play badly.

For boys, PE can reinforce traditional masculine ideals of strength and athleticism. Some may feel inadequate and weak if they don't live up to these.

WHAT YOU MIGHT BE THINKING

If you have bad memories of PE lessons, you may be tempted to give her an excuse. Alternatively, concern about obesity and screen-time among teens may mean you feel she should take part. If she complains about her weight—and you think she may have reason—you may think she should do PE.

WHAT SHE MIGHT BE THINKING

- **By now**, she's likely to see herself as either sporty or not sporty. If she feels she's the latter, she may believe there's no point in trying and that PE teachers favor athletic pupils.

- **She may dislike** the cramped or smelly changing rooms and fear that others will judge her body and compare development. If she wears makeup, she may not want to get sweaty or have to shower.

- **If she's fighting** against authority, she could resent the military-style PE directions and also won't want to be forced outside in the cold.

- **She may find** her gym outfit uncomfortable or embarrassing, especially if she has larger breasts.

- **Studies show that PE** is a main arena for intimidation and bullying. As physical confrontation is part of sports, teachers may not see the subtext of what's happening. If she feels scared, she may be too embarrassed to tell you.

HOW YOU COULD RESPOND

In the moment

Acknowledge her feelings
Ask her why she doesn't enjoy PE. This will help you brainstorm solutions and give you the opportunity to discuss the benefits of being active.

Suggest a sports buddy
Does she have a friend in her class who's at the same sports level as her? Suggest they team up so that they can support each other.

Help her feel equipped
Ask if her gym outfit fits or if there's anything that will make PE lessons more comfortable, such as extra deodorant or a sports bra.

Value PE lessons
Some parents dismiss PE lessons, sending the message that they're less important than other subjects. But research shows that engaging in sports improves concentration and social skills, as well as fitness.

In the long term

Don't be overly competitive
Emphasize effort, not results. Instead of talking about winning, make the goal having the opportunity to run around, get some fresh air, and raise her heart rate. Point out it's good to be physically challenged.

Be a good role model
Your children are more likely to exercise if other members of the family do so, too.

Say there's a sport for everyone
If she lacks confidence in her sports ability, she may find team sports daunting because of the fear of letting teammates down. Talk to her about other options for keeping fit, from yoga, to Zumba, to jogging and cycling.

Avoid "good" and "bad" labels
Just as hearing that others are good or bad at math can inform opinions on ability, teens may come to believe the same applies to sports. Explain that, as with any subject, she can get better at sports with practice and effort.

SEE RELATED TOPICS
I need a new bra: pp.60–61
He keeps picking on me: pp.62–63

"I'M NOT HUNGRY IN THE MORNING."

Breakfast is viewed as the most important meal of the day, but your teenager may have other ideas. Half of teenagers don't eat breakfast regularly before school because they say they don't have time to eat or they feel that it's not important.

SCENARIO | As he races off to school, your teen says he doesn't need breakfast.

Your teen may find it hard to get up on time because levels of the wake-up hormone, cortisol, rise later in the morning in adolescents than they do in adults. So he may often be running late, and the hormones that trigger hunger pangs won't have kicked in by the time he leaves.

Peer pressure may also play a part. He may be meeting friends before school to stop off at a convenience store or coffee shop to buy unsustaining snacks, energy drinks, and coffee. When hunger kicks in later in the morning, he may find it difficult to concentrate in class.

WHAT YOU MIGHT BE THINKING

As breakfast helps us focus, you may feel annoyed that he's not reaping its benefits. If he spends time on his appearance up to the last minute, you may feel even more frustrated.

WHAT HE MIGHT BE THINKING

◉ **When he wakes up**, he may be more interested in looking good for school than eating well. If he doesn't feel hungry, he won't see the point of wasting time.

◉ **His refusal to eat breakfast** may be a way to assert independence, making it clear he can make his own choices.

◉ **If you've had to nag him** to get up, breakfast is likely to feel like one more thing that you lecture him about. He'll probably insist he knows best how he feels—and what he needs.

◉ **If he's watching his weight**, he may be under the false impression that skipping a meal a day helps.

◀ **SEE RELATED TOPICS** ▶
Peer pressure and "FOMO": pp.58–59
Let me sleep!: pp.104–105

> **"**   **"**
> ## TEENS MAY FEEL THEY DON'T HAVE TIME FOR BREAKFAST OR THAT IT'S UNIMPORTANT.

HOW YOU COULD RESPOND

In the moment

Say you understand he's not hungry
If he genuinely isn't hungry because his hunger hormones haven't kicked in, offer grab-and-go food. Studies show that teens are more likely to eat breakfast if there are healthy to-go options available, such as bagels, smoothies, or granola bars. Get him involved by suggesting he prepares or sets them out the night before. If he doesn't eat them before class, he can put them in his backpack to eat later if hunger pangs strike.

Talk about it
Avoid making this a battleground. Ask him what time he does feel hungry and whether his concentration is affected if he has to wait for lunch. Say you're not trying to control what he does, but you're trying to help him feel and function as well as he can. Ask for his ideas about how to make mornings easier.

In the long term

Mention the benefits of breakfast
Discuss how studies show pupils who eat breakfast have improved focus, a healthier BMI, a more positive self-image, and better-smelling breath. Explain that an early meal with protein helps stabilize blood sugar levels, keeping hunger at bay so he doesn't overeat later on.

Make breakfast appealing
To stop breakfast from feeling like a chore, enjoy family breakfasts on weekends. Regular family mealtimes boost teens' self-worth. On weekends, make breakfast items such as muffins to freeze for the week ahead.

Discuss the downsides of caffeine
If he drinks energy drinks or coffee on the way to school, discuss how caffeine is a stimulant that can make him feel jittery by heightening the body's stress response. Many caffeine drinks also have high amounts of sugar, contributing to weight gain. Suggest healthier options.

"YOU'RE SO EMBARRASSING!"

Finding your parents embarrassing is part of the transition from childhood to adulthood. It helps if you see this as a necessary phase your teenager passes through rather than take it as a personal criticism.

SCENARIO | At a family party, your teen rolls her eyes, embarrassed, as you dance.

When your teen was a child, you had a lot of power over her. As her source of love and support, she put you on a pedestal. With growing independence, she may question your authority and find fault, often with the smallest detail, as she looks for reasons to break free. She's also highly egocentric now. This helps her develop a stronger sense of self but also means she thinks that all eyes are upon her, making her acutely self-conscious. This phase usually tapers off at 15–16 years old, as she gains more perspective.

WHAT YOU MIGHT BE THINKING

Being told you're embarrassing can feel hurtful, as we want our children to feel proud of us. You may also be irritated that you cannot enjoy yourself without being criticized.

WHAT SHE MIGHT BE THINKING

◉ **Your teen is working out** her place in the world by making comparisons and being more critical. As well as judging peers, she's likely to judge you.

◉ **Although she loves you**, she also has to paint you as imperfect to justify subconsciously the pain of separating from you.

◉ **She knows** that peers can judge others based on how cool, attractive, or wealthy their parents are. If you cross the social "norm" even slightly, she may be embarrassed by association.

◉ **She feels physically** uncomfortable if embarrassed. Brain scans show teens suffer more acute symptoms of a stress response, such as a raised heartbeat and sweaty palms, if they feel watched or judged.

SEE RELATED TOPICS
Communicating with teens: pp.46–47
Peer pressure and "FOMO": pp.58–59

" "

AS TEENAGERS WORK OUT THEIR PLACE IN THE WORLD, THEY MAKE COMPARISONS AND BECOME CRITICAL.

HOW YOU COULD RESPOND

In the moment

Accept it
Avoid taking her reaction personally. Accept that she'll find you embarrassing in some way.

Don't apologize
Stay true to yourself to teach her a healthy lesson about not sacrificing yourself to others' opinions. Although she's criticizing you, she also wants you to be worthy of her respect.

Stay calm
Teens often want to disown parents in social situations, so family parties can make her feel conflicted and hypersensitive. Acknowledge that while she feels judged, you don't and are comfortable having fun.

Distract her from her feelings
Quietly suggest she focuses on other activities or guests to shift her attention away from herself.

In the long term

Ask her to consider you
Part of our role is to help teens understand others' feelings. If you were upset, use "I feel" statements to explain gently how her comments were received by you.

Be patient
It can be painful to hear that your teen finds you embarrassing. However, try to hold firm, because once she has a stronger sense of self and perspective, she'll return to loving you just as you are.

Remember your childhood
Put her comments in perspective. You probably found your parents embarrassing at her age. Use humor to relay stories about them and how you once felt the same.

Be sensitive
Think how you would have felt as a teenager if your parents were doing what you're doing now. When possible, look for other opportunities to let your hair down when she isn't around.

"THIS IS **SO BORING**."

Now that your teenager has more control over his time, he's more likely to want to spend it how he wants. When he says he's bored, this is his way of saying to you, "I want to decide what I do and not to be told what I'm doing."

SCENARIO | While on vacation, you visit an art gallery. Once there, your teen complains that he doesn't find it interesting and is bored.

As teens pull away from parents, they want to show they're grown-up. Saying they find experiences you choose boring is a way to show independence.

Teens are also sensation seekers. Research shows they crave experiences that trigger the release of the feel-good hormone dopamine in the brain. This means, unless he's doing something exciting, he may be prone to boredom. He may also feel bored because he's used to constant stimulation on his phone. If you're trying to avoid devices on vacation, the real world may feel dull by comparison.

WHAT YOU MIGHT BE THINKING

You may hear his complaint as a personal rejection, when you've invested in this trip and hoped it would be happy family time. You may be annoyed because it feels like he's accusing you of not entertaining him.

WHAT HE MIGHT BE THINKING

⊚ **Adolescents tend to believe** their needs are the most important. He may think he's just being honest and hasn't realized that you may feel hurt when he says he's not enjoying time with you.

⊚ **If your relationship** is going through a difficult phase, saying he's bored may be his way of rejecting your values and interests and making it clear he has his own.

⊚ **If he uses his phone** as a default at any spare moment, he may find it hard to focus on activities that don't offer the same instant gratification. He may be interpreting his feelings of discomfort as boredom.

⊚ **Your teen may say** he's bored to express feeling ignored or disconnected from what's happening or to complain you're not paying attention to him. If he feels pressured to do well, he may see a gallery visit as your attempt to force-feed culture and history when he wants to unwind from schoolwork.

HOW YOU COULD RESPOND

In the moment

Acknowledge his views
Tell him you know it can feel uncomfortable to feel like he has nothing to do. Explain the boredom will soon pass and help him open up to the sights around him.

Ask him what he'd rather do
Stating what he would rather be doing can make it easier for him to accept the reality. Remind him you'll be doing lots of things he likes at other times on vacation.

Help him look beyond a screen
If he's usually preoccupied by his phone, you may feel that his complaining will ruin the visit and it's easier to let him go on it. However, next time he's bored, he'll expect the same, and it will be harder to say no. Put away your phones and present phone-free family time as a reward to help everyone relax.

Don't feel guilty
Studies show that teens are most likely to express boredom at this age; however, some downtime sparks the imagination. Not being highly entertained each minute allows him to think and feel in a less pressured way.

Use understanding and humor
He may be playing up to the role of the bored teen. Let him know in a light-hearted way that you see his viewpoint but that it's still good to be together.

In the long term

Think about your interactions
Are you leaving him to his own devices because you expect him to complain? Reaching out will help him feel included. Say you enjoy his company so he doesn't feel the need to test you.

Take action if he's often bored
Research suggests that high levels of boredom, especially in the early- to mid-teens, could be cause for concern because it can lead to teens taking risks with alcohol or drugs to create excitement and stimulation. If this is the case, invest more time in him. Think about his interests and suggest activities he'll enjoy.

SEE RELATED TOPICS
It's my phone: pp.96–97
You never listen: pp.118–119

"HE SHARED THIS PICTURE."

During the teenage years, young people are discovering sexual desire and gauging how attractive they are. Estimates vary, but these factors may lead as many as one in four teens to "sext"—send intimate selfies or videos—usually to someone they're attracted to.

SCENARIO | Your teen is crying because she's discovered that her ex has shown a nude picture she sent him to his friends.

As teenagers spend a lot of time online, it's natural that they'll flirt online, too. In early adolescence, they're also impulsive. Digital technology not only makes it easy to take sexual pictures of themselves, but also to send such images at the touch of a button—before they've thought through the risks.

While most sexts are sent and received privately between two people, in about 12 percent of cases, images get forwarded—either accidentally or purposely—and seen by others. Often, they may be shared by the other teen who sees receiving a sext as a trophy that will impress friends.

WHAT YOU MIGHT BE THINKING

You may be shocked that she sent an erotic image and disappointed and angry that she would be so irresponsible. You might also be furious with the boy and want to stop it from spreading.

WHAT SHE MIGHT BE THINKING

⊙ **If your daughter** was asked to send the image, she may have felt as if she had little choice. That's because if she doesn't send one, she may fear being labeled as frigid, a bitch, or a prude.

⊙ **She may have been** dipping her toe into expressing her sexuality. If she's insecure about her body, she may have sent it because she could airbrush parts of her body, making her feel more in control and desirable.

⊙ **If she sent the image** to a boy she liked or was seeing to create a bond of trust, she's likely to be devastated at his betrayal.

⊙ **She'll wish the drama** would magically disappear. She's probably telling you only because she fears you'll hear about it from another source and because she needs adult help to remove the image.

◀ **SEE RELATED TOPICS** ▶
We're going out together: pp.170–171
Consent: pp.196–197

> **TECHNOLOGY MEANS THAT THE PROCESS OF EXPLORING SEXUALITY CAN NOW BE EASILY MADE PUBLIC.**

HOW YOU COULD RESPOND

In the moment

Avoid shaming
Teenagers have always wanted to explore their sexuality, but technology has made that process more public. Your teen knows she's been reckless. Making her feel worse will deter her from seeking help in future. Instead, say you understand she feels betrayed and assure her we've all done things we've regretted. Unless she says it's okay, don't ask to see the image. Telling you will be one of the worst parts of the experience.

Act fast to stop the picture from spreading
Contact the teen she sent it to as soon as possible, even if she's horrified by this action. Tell them to delete it and to tell anyone they shared it with to do so. Point out it's illegal to share sexual images of anyone under the age of 18. If you believe it's been uploaded to public social networks or photo-sharing sites, alert these platforms. Make it clear that it's a nude image of a minor so they act quickly to take it down.

In the long term

Discuss standing up to unwanted pressure
If her ex told her that "everyone shares pictures," statistics show this isn't true. If she doesn't want to sext, tell her it's fine to say no. If a boy pressures her in the future, it means he's not to be trusted with an intimate picture.

Ask her to use the "Grandma" test
In the future, if she wants to send a risqué picture, suggest she runs through a mental checklist, such as "Could this get me or the recipient in trouble and could it be shared?" and "Would I mind my grandma seeing it?" This may help her think again.

Talk about harm reduction
Research shows that teens increasingly limit sexting to trusting romantic relationships, and for many, it's part of modern relationships. Talk about how to limit the risks by avoiding identifiable settings, covering up distinctive body markings, and keeping her hands and face out of view.

SELF-HARM

Self-harm is one of the ways some teenagers release overwhelming emotions. By making pain physical rather than emotional, they experience temporary relief and feel in control again.

There are many forms of self-harm, including cutting, self-bruising, burning, pinching, scratching, punching walls, and hair-pulling. Risky behavior such as taking drugs, having unsafe sex, binge-drinking, or eating too little or too much can also be self-harming behaviors in girls and boys. Triggers can include loneliness, self-hatred, relationship breakdown, and isolation. Teens may also punish themselves for not being "good enough," or they may want others to see their distress, though usually it's hidden. Whatever the reason, quick intervention is key so self-harm doesn't become their way to cope.

" "

MAKING PAIN PHYSICAL RATHER THAN EMOTIONAL PROVIDES TEMPORARY RELIEF FOR SOME.

1
Trust your instinct
If you suspect self-harming, start a conversation in which your teen feels they can talk freely and be heard without judgment.

4
Say to seek help for a friend
If a friend sends pictures or shows them their cuts, tell your teen they must tell an adult. This is too much for teenagers to handle alone.

6
Explore emotions
Help them talk openly, no matter how hard. Discuss healthy ways in which you cope with difficult feelings.

9
Remove the methods
Put sharp objects high up and hide scissors so teens have to search, giving time for impulsive feelings to pass.

WORKING THINGS OUT

10 key principles

2
React calmly
Avoid showing anger or hurt. Assure them you love them, even if you don't understand. Don't make them promise to stop, as this adds to shameful feelings of being "messed up."

3
Talk about their peers
Self-harm can spread quickly through friendship groups. Discuss how it's a way of saying, "Help me, I feel out of control." Discuss how it's better to relieve feelings in less risky ways.

5
Suggest physical alternatives
Replacement behavior such as squeezing an ice cube, drawing on skin, or taking a cold shower can help break self-harm cycles. Writing down feelings, talking to a safe person, or a diverting activity can also help.

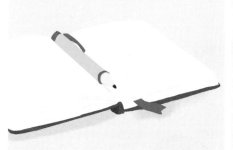

7
Suggest a therapist
Teens who find it hard to open up to parents may express themselves more freely to a counselor. Offer to find one to help them cope.

8
Discuss social media
This can normalize and romanticize self-harming. Unfollowing self-harming accounts and limiting social media use helps protect teens.

10
Explain that relief is temporary
When the body is cut, it responds by producing endorphins, natural pain relievers that give temporary relief. It's important to help teens understand that while they may feel better in the moment, this isn't an effective long-term coping method, as it feeds back into feelings of shame and guilt and makes these worse. While the pain will pass, scars will last.

TAILORED ADVICE

Age by age

13–14
YEAR-OLDS

Stick to bedtimes
Don't abandon bedtimes. Tired teens find it harder to regulate emotions and so are at more risk of self-harm.

Share coping strategies
By 14, a fifth of girls have self-harmed. Talk about healthy coping strategies to keep your teen from copying friends.

15–16
YEAR-OLDS

Notice risky behavior
With more freedom and academic pressure, teens may turn to binge-drinking or reckless sex to discharge pressure.

Be alert around test times
Pressure can trigger self-harm. Suggest other ways to release tension, such as going for a run.

17–18
YEAR-OLDS

Stay close
Talk and listen. Some older teens believe others won't take their feelings seriously unless they self-harm.

Seek services when away
If your teen still self-harms, link them to counseling services at college.

"I DIDN'T SLAM THE DOOR!"

Just like toddlers, teens have volatile emotions that can lead to temper tantrums. Now that they're bigger and stronger, these outbursts are more intimidating. As you once helped her learn to control her impulses when she was younger, she may need your help to manage angry emotions now.

SCENARIO | Your teen storms off and slams the door following a fight.

Your teen may look grown-up, but the frontal lobe of her brain, which regulates self-control, is still developing. The part of the brain called the amygdala, which is sensitive to the effects of hormones, is also quicker to excite primal fight-or-flight responses. All of this means she finds it hard to contain outbursts and reacts more emotionally and less logically in disputes.

If she feels overwhelmed, ignored, or that she can't win, slamming the door feels like the most impactful way to have the last word.

WHAT YOU MIGHT BE THINKING

If she was rude, you may want to follow her to tell her to listen. You may worry she's damaged the door or walls and feel she has no respect for you or her home. If she lashed out physically, you may want to avoid crossing her again.

WHAT SHE MIGHT BE THINKING

◉ **You may see** slamming the door as attacking your authority, but she's likely to see it as an acceptable way to end a conversation she knows she can't win. She knows you won't like this action, so it's also her way of saying she doesn't always accept your authority.

◉ **Releasing her pent-up** emotion into one physical gesture feels satisfying and like the best way to show how upset she is and get rid of the build-up of tension she's been feeling.

◉ **Your teen senses** if she lost her temper with friends, they wouldn't stick around. She feels secure expressing anger with you because she knows you'll always be there for her. Studies show that while parents see arguments with teens as destructive, teens see them as constructive if they get heard.

◉ **A temper tantrum** aimed at you may be a safe way of letting off tension about another issue, such as a friendship one, which may not come to light until later on.

HOW YOU COULD RESPOND

In the moment

Don't follow
Allowing her to retreat to her room helps her calm down and process her thoughts.

Keep control
If you feel your fight-or-flight reaction kicking in, walk away. Shouting to restore authority or issuing threats will make her more emotionally reactive and teach her that's how to deal with anger. Model staying calm, using strategies such as counting down from 20 or taking slow breaths.

Stick to the point
By drawing you into a fight, she may be trying to distract you from an issue. Give her space to regain her logical thinking. When she's ready to talk, calmly repeat both sides of the argument so she knows you've listened.

Help her manage her anger
Explain anger is a natural emotion, neither right nor wrong, but she can choose how to communicate it. Point out aggression will never help get her view across.

In the long term

Spot signs and triggers
Ask her to watch for signs of anger, such as shallow breaths and muscle tension. If she spots these, she could walk away. Without blame, discuss triggers. Ask her to brainstorm solutions to avoid conflict so she feels heard.

Hold the line
She may sense you feel afraid to cross her. Ensure she knows you stand firm and united with your co-parent, especially where issues of health and safety are concerned.

Introduce consequences
If she caused damage, ask her to help pay for repairs out of her allowance. Don't consider removing her door! It's important she retains her privacy.

Spend one-on-one time with her
Teens can react in anger when they feel overwhelmed, powerless, or criticized. Spend time with her. The more you talk, the more likely you'll get to the bottom of issues that might be bothering her.

◤ **SEE RELATED TOPICS** ◢
I hate you!: pp.44–45
You never listen: pp.118–119

"I'M NOT GOING TO SCHOOL."

Every teenager complains about going to school at some point. However, if your child refuses to go, it can turn into a power struggle, generating conflicting feelings—especially if you need to get to work. Help him unravel his reasons.

SCENARIO | Your teen refuses to get dressed and go to school.

There are a range of reasons why your teen may refuse to go to school. He may have fallen behind with work, be worried about a test, or be scared of being told off. If he's lagging behind academically or has an undiagnosed learning difficulty, he may be so disheartened that he feels like giving up. It's also possible that he's struggling socially. He may be scared of facing the fallout from a fight or feel he has no friends and is worried about having no one to eat lunch with.

Whatever the reason, school refusal may be a last resort to express his unhappiness. Your goal is to help him feel more empowered and in control of what happens to him.

WHAT YOU MIGHT BE THINKING

You may feel resentful at the fights and powerless if he's noncommunicative or angry. You may worry he'll fall behind and be exasperated because school is a legal requirement and you could be fined.

WHAT HE MIGHT BE THINKING

⊚ **Your teen may want** to go to school, but if he has anxiety issues, home may feel like a safer option than school.

⊚ **He may find it hard** to identify and talk about emotions. When young people struggle this way, they can feel emotional pain as a physical sensation. For example, stress may manifest as headaches, anxiety as stomachaches, and sadness as backaches.

⊚ **He may feel aggressive** toward you if he feels that his refusal is simply inconvenient to you. He may struggle to express his unhappiness and might think that you're not interested.

⊚ **He may be exhausted**. Teens who refuse to go to school may have slipped out of healthy sleep routines. If he's up late on a device, this will make him irritable and reactive in the mornings.

HOW YOU COULD RESPOND

In the moment

Look forward
Tell him gently but firmly that he needs to go to school today, but you'd like to talk about his reasons later. Be clear that the school could take action against you if he stops going. Explain that avoidance will make it harder to return. Say you believe he can do this.

Manage your worry
Let the school know that he may be late and tell work you're behind schedule. If he continues to refuse, arrange a flexible working day or ask a family member or friend to stay with him to keep him off devices. If he's developed a pattern of refusal, be honest with the school. Research shows that working with the school helps address issues more quickly.

Help him look forward
Focus on something positive you'll do later. Make it clear it's not shameful to worry about school, it's how he deals with it that matters.

In the long term

Set a routine
He's more likely to refuse to go to school if he's sleep-deprived, most likely from looking at devices at night. Talk about stopping using his phone an hour before bedtime to help him sleep and improve well-being.

School anxiety is often caused by worries building up and won't improve overnight.

Check other symptoms
If he's experiencing panic attacks, he may need to discuss the triggers with a professional.

Give positive reinforcement
When he does go to school, chat about how it went. Acknowledge his feelings and emphasize how he coped. Talk about how you dealt with an anxiety. Be patient.

Help find solutions
Use a problem-solving approach to break down his anxiety into small steps with clear solutions—whether to help him catch up or to deal with social or other issues.

" "

SCHOOL REFUSAL CAN BE A TEENAGER'S LAST RESORT TO EXPRESS UNHAPPINESS.

SEE RELATED TOPICS
I skipped lunch: pp.54–55
Everyone gets better grades than me: pp.66–67

"SOMEONE HAS TAGGED ME IN A HORRIBLE PICTURE."

At this age, girls in particular use social media platforms to vie for social status, which can lead them to post mean comments or pictures. Use such incidents to coach your teen on how to deal with social cruelty.

SCENARIO | A friend tagged your teen in an unflattering picture from a party.

In early adolescence, when teens are most insecure, they can ruthlessly use photos, friend status updates, comments, and block and unfollow buttons on social media to establish pecking order. Tagging others in pictures or labeling a picture with their name is another way to show who's in or out of friendship groups. Tagging can also post unflattering pictures of a rival or former friend. Instead of insulting words, which can land teens in trouble with adults, tagging is an under-the-radar way to embarrass peers. If accused of meanness, they may say the person is sensitive or that it was a joke.

WHAT YOU MIGHT BE THINKING

You may be unsure about how to respond if the teen who posted is an on–off friend. You may want to protect your teen but think she should toughen up and spend less time on social media.

◆ **SEE RELATED TOPICS** ▶

She's such a bitch!: pp.50–51
Friendship issues: pp.64–65

WHAT SHE MIGHT BE THINKING

◉ **Your daughter probably** curates her online image carefully, so she can feel angry and out of control if she thinks her peers are laughing at an embarrassing picture she wouldn't have posted.

◉ **Teens already feel** watched by an imaginary audience. On social media, she may believe everyone has seen the picture and feel very anxious. She's probably monitoring reactions to see who comments on the photo.

◉ **She may be embarrassed** telling you because she wants to keep up appearances in front of you.

◉ **She wants the situation** to end. She may be scared you'll intervene on her behalf, worsening the fight. She also worries you might remove her phone.

" "
TEENS CAN USE SOCIAL MEDIA PLATFORMS TO BATTLE FOR SOCIAL STATUS.

HOW YOU COULD RESPOND

In the moment

Consider both sides of the story
Research shows that most of this behavior takes place between teens who know each other, and each other's weak spots, well. Ask gently if there's more to the story.

Be supportive
Though important, the instability of teen friendships means it's vital parents stay connected so they are a source of support. Don't remove her phone. She'll be more anxious if she can't monitor what's being said or contact friends. Teens' egocentricity means they often overestimate the attention others pay to them. Remind her that she doesn't personally know many of her followers and that they're not taking as much notice as she thinks.

Discuss standing up for herself
Show her how to convey that she's not an easy target. Take a screenshot, help her untag herself, then brainstorm ways to calmly ask the girl to remove it.

In the long term

Put the incident in context
Rather than assume it's bullying, which is repetitive and designed to harm, talk to her about conflict as a normal part of social interaction and how it's better to learn to deal with it assertively. Say that social cruelty is common in teens so she doesn't feel like she's the only one affected.

Map out the dynamics
Understanding the roles of aggressors, targets, and bystanders (who watch and say nothing) within peer groups equips her to spot behavior patterns and not take it so personally. If the person who posted is an on–off friend or "frenemy" who veers between being friendly and mean, could she focus on peers who don't behave in this way?

Suggest she puts boundaries on her social media use
Research shows that a maximum of an hour a day on social media is enough time to stay in touch but not long enough to be dragged into online power struggles.

"**I HATE** WRITING HOMEWORK ESSAYS."

Parents hope that their children will study hard at school so they have more choices when they leave. However, as work builds up, you may become increasingly frustrated if your teen doesn't appear to be putting in the work she needs to do well.

SCENARIO | When it's close to bedtime, you check whether your teen has finished her essay. She says she has, but she's barely written a page.

You may be tempted to think your teen is being lazy, but there can be many underlying reasons why she doesn't appear to be putting in her best effort.

If she has been made to feel she's not doing well, she may be trying to protect herself. While some teens respond to academic pressure by putting more effort in, others think they'll fail anyway, so it feels safer not to try. Another reason she may seem to not be trying is if there's an underlying learning issue making schoolwork hard and uncomfortable.

WHAT YOU MIGHT BE THINKING

You may feel angry, thinking that she's lazy, and wonder why she cannot make more effort. You may be tired of pestering her about work but at a loss as to how to motivate her, as nothing seems to work. You may also worry about her future.

WHAT SHE MIGHT BE THINKING

⦿ **She may not see** the point of hard work yet. While parents see the long-term benefits of success, to a teen still developing the brain's executive functions of self-discipline and goal-setting, schoolwork is just another thing grown-ups tell her to do.

⦿ **Your teen may not have** the self-discipline to meet increasing demands. She might think either that she's not smart and sees no point in trying or that she's so smart she can coast for a bit longer.

⦿ **She may not try hard** if her peer group believes it's uncool to work hard. She may be more eager to follow their interests to fit in with them.

⦿ **She may be tired** after school. If she's then distracted by devices, she may not get down to work in time to do a good job.

⦿ **If she feels nagged**, this is likely to make her resentful. She may become secretive or claim that she's doing what's required, or just as much as everyone else, to get you off her back.

HOW YOU COULD RESPOND

In the moment

Don't call her lazy
This won't motivate her. Labeling her will only contribute to any feelings of shame or resentment, and she'll protect herself by shutting down further and becoming secretive about her schoolwork.

Avoid telling her to hurry up
If she has an underlying learning issue, putting pressure on her could make her go into fight-flight-freeze mode, which slows down the logical part of her brain.

Help her plan
She's liable to be less daunted and write more if she plans out the focus of her essay. Also, show her how to draw a mind map, with a question in the middle and ideas branching out, to help her think more clearly.

Don't offer bribes
If you offer money for a certain grade, this can undermine her internal motivation because she's pleasing you rather than starting to want to please herself.

In the long term

Talk about what's in it for her
Ask where she would like to be in 1, 3, and 5 years and help her see how short-term steps lead to long-term goals. Working out herself what she needs to do develops "intrinsic" motivation.

Discuss her feelings
Rather than react to conflicts at parents' evenings or after tests, chat when you're both calm. Does she see no point in trying or think she doesn't need to? Is she afraid of doing well in front of peers? What are her strengths and weaknesses? Help her bring her fears to the fore to deal with them.

Get an assessment
If she struggles to focus and finish work on time, there may be an underlying issue, such as slow processing of information. Identifying this can help.

Talk about a growth mindset
If she lacks academic confidence, explain how the right techniques and practices can train her brain to improve. Let her find her own goals that will stretch her to her limits, whether it's running a 10k, hiking up a mountain, or raising money for charity. Setting a goal and sticking to it is more likely to predict success in life than high grades.

▶ **SEE RELATED TOPICS** ◀
I've got too much to do: pp.52–53
I am studying: pp.128–129

"I SAW **THIS PICTURE.**"

While the internet is an unparalleled learning tool that gives teenagers instant access to a vast collection of knowledge and information, it also makes unwanted exposure to sexually graphic, violent, or disturbing material much more likely.

SCENARIO | Your teen is upset when he clicks on a link titled "this will make you laugh" and instead views images of an animal being tortured.

When it comes to teens being exposed to disturbing or inappropriate material online, unfortunately it's a matter of "when," not "if." There are several ways your teen can view such content. Curiosity about sex may lead him to extreme pornography. He may also be sent links to images of violence, gore, or suicide, or stumble on pictures of self-harm on social media.

One of the most common is distressing videos of animal cruelty, which have been seen by about a quarter of adolescents, sometimes sent via links with misleading titles. Once seen, visual memories are harder to forget. As traumatic memories are processed differently from nontraumatic ones, images may randomly pop into your teen's head for months after.

WHAT YOU MIGHT BE THINKING

You might worry that what is seen cannot be unseen and that this may shake his view of the world as a safe place. You may struggle to explain the cruelty or to put it in perspective.

WHAT HE MIGHT BE THINKING

⊙ **If he clicked on a link** without realizing what the content would be, your teenager may feel upset or stupid for falling for this, as well as angry with the person who sent the link to him.

⊙ **If he found the image** because he was curious, he may feel self-blame for inflicting this disturbing imagery on himself. He may worry that you will restrict his internet access.

⊙ **Your teen may struggle** to rationalize how humans can behave toward animals with such cruelty, and it may chip away at his faith in the goodness of people.

⊙ **Your teen may already** have tried to manage his worry by trying not to think about what he saw but may have found the image keeps reappearing in his mind. It may pop into his head now every time he closes his eyes or tries to concentrate.

◄ **SEE RELATED TOPICS** ►
Social media: pp.38–39
Talking about pornography: pp.150–151

" "

DISTURBING OR
INAPPROPRIATE ONLINE
MATERIAL IS ALL TOO
EASILY VIEWED OR
STUMBLED UPON
BY TEENAGERS.

HOW YOU COULD RESPOND

In the moment

Listen openly
Thank him for telling you. Listening to his experience and feelings without judgment is more likely to encourage him to seek your help the next time he's upset.

Talk about it
You may worry that talking about it keeps the image alive, but it's far better for him to process it with the benefit of your adult perspective than try to deal with it on his own.

Report it
Part of his distress is that he feels powerless to prevent the cruelty. Point out that he can help by taking steps to report it. Animal rights' groups recommend downloading the images and getting a copy of the link rather than just taking a screenshot for evidence. They also advise collecting as many details as you can about the account and reporting it to animal welfare organizations and law enforcement agencies.

In the long term

Give perspective
After the immediate shock, help him rationalize the experience. Talk about how a small amount of extreme material is circulated on the internet by a small group of people for shock value—and such incidents of animal cruelty are rare. Reassure him that the majority of people do not act like this. Learning not to react to them starves them of attention and entertainment.

Explain it may take time
Tell him that while the shock will fade, it could take up to 6 months for the image to leave his mind. Help him replace the images in his head. Talk about how the brain has limited focus and can hold only so many thoughts at one time. Say he can replace the negative image by exposing his brain to more positive images, such as videos of animals being lovingly cared for.

"I'M SO HAIRY."

Teenagers have always felt self-conscious and worried about being judged by their looks. However, with more images of physical perfection on social media, teens tend to hold themselves up to much higher standards of personal grooming than in the past—including hair removal.

SCENARIO | Your teen asks if she can get her legs and bikini line waxed.

Throughout history, body hair has been one of the most visible markers of gender, and it has been seen as feminine for women to have less body hair than men. Over recent years, teenage girls increasingly believe they should have no body hair at all, and a growing number of teens are waxing. This is partly due to the way women are shown in pornography. The growth in hair-removal salons, and the norms set by celebrities and online personalities, may also have given your teen the idea that it's "unclean" or unfeminine to have any body hair.

WHAT YOU MIGHT BE THINKING

You may have conflicted feelings. You may think she's too young to get onto this expensive, painful, and time-consuming treadmill. At the same time, you don't want her to feel embarrassed or to be teased about how she looks.

" "

IMAGES OF PERFECTION ON SOCIAL MEDIA ENCOURAGE HIGH LEVELS OF GROOMING.

WHAT SHE MIGHT BE THINKING

⊙ **Your teen may be** avoiding wearing a bikini for fear others will see she has hair around her bikini line. She may have heard waxing is the best way to get longer-lasting hair removal.

⊙ **Having a smooth**, hair-free body may make her feel better about her body—as if she can instantly achieve the standards of grooming and perfection portrayed by today's celebrities.

⊙ **She may not** have been teased, but she may have seen others whispering about girls who have visible hair, and she's desperate to avoid being singled out by peers for the same reason.

⊙ **She may believe** that having visible hairs makes her look ungroomed or even dirty to others. She may have observed your hair-removal ritual and sees this as a rite of passage.

HOW YOU COULD RESPOND

In the moment

Acknowledge her feelings
Rather than dismiss her request, ask her why she wants waxing. Ask if she knows how it feels and offer to try a small wax strip on her leg at home to see if she feels it's worth it.

Talk about the cost
Is she ready for the high cost in time and money of staying waxed? Shaving is less costly, and she can be more in charge of her hair removal. If she still wants waxing, suggest she does extra household chores to contribute to the cost.

Discuss the benefits of hair
Chat about the reasons we naturally have pubic hair—as a cushion to protect the area against friction and bacteria. Say that complete removal brings risks, such as hair follicle infections, which can lead to cysts.

In the long term

Talk about opposing views
Mention how some women resist cultural messages by dying their underarm and crotch hair bright colors so she sees there are alternatives. Ask her to consider why most men don't feel pressure to endure painful hair removal processes and how society perpetuates and reinforces beauty standards that can harm women.

Help her be herself
She may not be ready to stand out from the crowd, but tell her there may be a time when she decides she doesn't care how others judge her body. If she decides to remove hair, she should do it for herself, not for others. Whatever she decides is okay.

SEE RELATED TOPICS
Can I skip PE?: pp.68–69
All my friends look amazing: pp.122–123

"SHE'S A **SLUT**."

A teenage girl's status can rise when she starts to be noticed and have relationships with boys, but it can also fall. If her peers think she's getting too much attention, that girl may be targeted and put down with words such as "slut."

SCENARIO | While giving your teen and a friend a lift, your daughter calls a classmate a slut. You ask her about this in the car, and bring it up again at home.

As teenagers become sexually aware, competition who is the most attractive sharpens. Girls believe that having a boyfriend makes them look more attractive and mature, but it may trigger jealous feelings in peers, who also want attention from boys. Jealousy can feel uncomfortable, so teens may justify their complex feelings by latching onto deeply embedded cultural ideas about "good" versus "bad" girls. Younger teens are also impulsive and still learning the impact of name-calling. It's likely that your teen doesn't grasp this word's full implications. She just knows it's a powerful way to bring down the reputation of a girl who's seen, consciously or not, as a rival.

WHAT YOU MIGHT BE THINKING

You may be shocked your daughter is undermining other girls by using sexist language. You may wonder where her strong views on other people's private lives come from.

WHAT SHE MIGHT BE THINKING

◉ **Your teen knows** this is one of the harshest insults available, but by calling a schoolmate a slut, she defines herself as a "good" girl by comparison. She's implying that she's a morally superior, more valuable young woman who is saving herself for the right person.

◉ **Taking the moral high ground** by calling another girl names may make her feel better about the fact that she may not yet have had interest from boys.

◉ **She may not** fully understand the word's meaning but knows it's a strong insult that could destroy another girl's reputation, bringing her down in the social hierarchy.

◉ **Although she's calling** another girl a slut, she may worry about being called it, too. When she gets dressed for a party, she may feel she has to tread a fine line between looking attractive and being seen as trying too hard.

◆ **SEE RELATED TOPICS** ◆
She's such a bitch!: pp.50–51
Friendship issues: pp.64–65

> **"IT'S LIKELY THAT YOUR DAUGHTER DOESN'T UNDERSTAND THE FULL IMPLICATION OF THIS INSULT.**

HOW YOU COULD RESPOND

In the moment

Intervene
You may be shocked by her language, but ask about her choice of words. By saying nothing, you tacitly condone her use of this term. Without criticizing, tell her you'd like to understand why she described a classmate in this way.

Talk about its effect
Once you've listened, explain your adult perspective. Say how slurs such as "slut" dehumanize and imply someone is worthless. Slut may also be used in sexual bullying by boys against girls, who may feel unable to escape the label.

Discuss gossip
We all exchange information about others, but it crosses a line if it's unproven or deliberately hurts. If the girl entered into a sexual relationship and now feels used, how would she feel about being called a slut? If your daughter heard negative gossip, how does she know it's true? Would she say this to the girl's face?

In the long term

Discuss gender politics
Talk about how competition for male attention can damage friendships. Ask why she thinks there's no equivalent word for boys and why girls are shamed but boys praised for sexual activity. Talk about how boys may be brought down in different ways, for example, with insults such as "weak" and "sissy," but that sexual insults are more commonly directed at women.

Ask her to think about pressures acting on her
Use this as a chance to talk about pressures she may encounter when she decides to be sexually active. How will she recognize and stand up to them?

Keep talking
Watch age-appropriate films together that explore how society judges women for their sexuality and desire in a way men are not. Discuss these messages.

"EVERYONE ELSE PLAYS THIS COMPUTER GAME."

For many boys, there are few activities more important to them—and their friendships—than video gaming. So if your son claims he's feeling left out by not being allowed to play a game meant for an older age group, you may wonder whether to bend the rules.

SCENARIO | Your teen is upset that you won't buy him a video game rated mature.

Multiplayer games played side-by-side and remotely with friends have become a key part of teenagers' social lives. However, you may be unnerved by the graphic violence of many games, with your teen often called upon to do the killing. Furthermore, such games reinforce male stereotypes, casting your son in the role of an unfeeling, merciless dominator.

WHAT YOU MIGHT BE THINKING

You may be disturbed by the graphic realism but want to keep him from feeling left out. Knowing his friends' parents apparently let their sons play may make you wonder if you're too strict. You may also worry that time spent gaming is at the expense of other activities.

66 99

VIDEO GAMES FEATURE STRONGLY IN THE FRIENDSHIPS OF TEENAGE BOYS.

WHAT HE MIGHT BE THINKING

◉ **Your teen believes** that being skilled at video games—and being able to talk about the latest release—boosts his social status. Even if only one or two of his friends have the game, in his mind, that's "everybody."

◉ **If you haven't played** video games with him, he's likely to believe you aren't qualified to judge what's safe for him.

◉ **Telling him that you're worried** that some games normalize violence is likely to make him defensive. He'll claim the games he's played haven't harmed him or his friends.

◉ **If you've given in** on this issue before, he believes he can wear you down.

SEE RELATED TOPICS
Just one more game: pp.130–131
Dad said I could: pp.154–155

HOW YOU COULD RESPOND

In the moment

Listen to his reasons
Ask him why he wants the game, which friends have it, why he believes it's rated mature, and why he thinks he should have it now. He may realize his case isn't as strong as he thinks.

Stand your ground
Giving in may lead him to assume that rules on issues such as drinking also don't apply. Although he's likely to shower you with gratitude if you agree, he's also likely to lose some respect for you. Say that keeping up with friends isn't a sufficient reason for ignoring age guidelines.

Decide on your values
Mature video games can normalize violence, humiliation, and torture and feature sexist stereotypes and brutal language. Let him know that while other parents may be okay with their teens playing an active character in such scenes, you aren't.

In the long term

Find out more
Playing video games with him will mean he'll respect your opinion more. You'll also gauge the level of violence he's seen.

Discuss physical symptoms
Realistic video games increase levels of fight-or-flight hormones such as cortisol. Say that if his heart starts racing or his palms get sweaty, it's a sign that he could be experiencing unnecessary stress.

Consider other risks
Tell him that with mature games, he's more likely to hear racist, homophobic, and strong language from older players, and there's a higher risk he'll be trolled.

Unite with responsible adults
Recruit the help of like-minded parents in staying firm. If your partner is more lenient, discuss the matter out of your son's hearing and form a united front.

"IT'S **MY PHONE**."

Half of teens admit feeling "addicted" to their phones, according to research—and 60 percent of parents agree that this is the case. So if you try to introduce limits, you may find your teen reacts aggressively and says you have no right.

SCENARIO | When your teen seems unable to put her phone away at family meals, you say you'll take it away.

Your teen may resent your interference for many reasons. Her phone connects her to her peers, so taking it away may trigger intense feelings of FOMO—fear of missing out. Also, at this age, her brain is very sensitive to the release of the feel-good chemical dopamine, so constant messages and pictures give her brain the reward it craves.

There isn't a recognized smartphone addiction diagnosis. However, if she uses her phone at the expense of other activities—such as face-to-face interaction, homework, and sleep—and is angry, impatient, and irritable when away from it, you may worry. Around a fifth of parents say they argue with their teen daily about phone use.

WHAT YOU MIGHT BE THINKING

If your teen reacts aggressively to a threat to confiscate her phone, you may worry she's addicted. You may be shocked by her reaction and angry that she acts like she owns the phone if you bought it and pay its monthly bill.

WHAT SHE MIGHT BE THINKING

⊚ **Your teen thinks** that everyone has a smartphone, so she believes that having one with her constantly is her basic human right—and that it's your duty to provide a phone, in the same way you do food, drink, and shelter.

⊚ **Your teen's phone** is her social life. Having it with her is like carrying around her friends. It's also her music playlist, camera, news source, and entertainment system, all rolled into one.

⊚ **Unless you clearly monitor her**, she probably feels she has almost total control over how she uses her phone. Your interference feels like a violation of her independence and privacy.

⊚ **She may have reached** a point where nothing else feels as interesting as what happens on her phone, including reading a book or going outside. When you take it away, she may feel at a loss.

◀ **SEE RELATED TOPICS** ▶
I need a new phone: pp.30–31
Peer pressure and "FOMO": pp.58–59

" "
YOUR TEENAGER'S PHONE IS A GATEWAY TO HER SOCIAL WORLD.

HOW YOU COULD RESPOND

In the moment

Understand its place in her life
When you take her phone away, it feels like you take away her social life, too. Removal won't help her learn how to manage its use, but it makes her desperate to keep control of it.

Draw clear boundaries
She probably feels she owns and controls her phone. Be clear that as the bill-paying adult, you have a say and that, at the least, you'd like to check privacy settings occasionally. She'll earn trust through responsible use.

Ask her to notice how her phone affects her
Explain that the notifications are designed to keep her checking her phone. Ask your teen to notice the buzz she gets when she receives a new message. Suggest she sees how long she can go without checking it and, if she goes for an hour, has she really missed anything?

In the long term

Help her spot signs of overuse
Can she look for symptoms such as eye strain, back pain, low mood, or irritability? Suggest an app that helps her become conscious of how she uses her phone.

Be a good role model
Spend phone-free time with her. Model moderate phone behavior by not responding immediately to texts and calls.

Introduce a digital sunset
Place a limit of no phones for everyone an hour before bedtime because the blue hue emitted by phones interferes with sleep hormones.

Suggest she thinks through the pros and cons
Do the pros (the convenience) outweigh the cons (constant comparison on social media)? Talk about research that shows the more she uses it, the more likely she is to come into conflict with peers and feel stressed.

"I'M GOING TO THE MARCH."

As your teen starts to develop his identity, he's able to look around him and think about his place in society. He can also think in more abstract ways about his future and what he can do to make the world a better place.

SCENARIO | Your teen says he wants to go to a protest march.

By this age, your teenager's brain is getting better at weighing evidence and analyzing it, which means he's developing the ability to see the bigger picture and where he fits in.

He's starting to see himself as a citizen of the wider world, looking beyond his own peer group to the bigger community that he wants to belong to.

He may be starting to wrestle with big issues such as the meaning of life and what his priorities are. For this reason, he is looking for causes to care about, latching onto new ideas, and starting to define himself by his beliefs. As he becomes aware of wider social issues, he may look for ways to express his views.

WHAT YOU MIGHT BE THINKING

How you feel about him joining a march depends on how far his beliefs align with yours and the value you place on the cause. If his interest is recent, you may wonder if he just wants to go with friends. You may worry he's too young and will get lost in a crowd or get hurt if it's chaotic.

66 99
YOUR TEEN IS STARTING TO SEE HIMSELF AS A CITIZEN OF THE WORLD.

WHAT HE MIGHT BE THINKING

⊙ **As a child**, your teen learned that adults are the experts. Now, he enjoys the fact that his voice also counts because the protest is about his future. Expressing his views on social media is likely to make him feel more emboldened.

⊙ **Whatever cause** he's interested in, civic engagement gives him a sense of belonging and identity. He also feels safe and accepted among other young people who echo his beliefs.

⊙ **Fourteen is the age** when social researchers have found teen rebellion against adult authority peaks, so standing up to it on a large scale appeals.

⊙ **He'll tend to believe** that adults have got it wrong and that he and his generation have the fresh eyes to see what needs to be done.

HOW YOU COULD RESPOND

In the moment

See it as a positive
Being involved with social protest is a sign of healthy development in adolescence. It can also help the formation of his identity and enhance cognitive and interpersonal skills.

Help him clarify his views
Listen to and discuss his views with an open mind—not to test him, but so that he can be clear about his facts, why he's engaged, and learn to weigh and evaluate the evidence.

Suggest alternatives
Discuss other ways he can be a good citizen at a local level by keeping abreast of community issues and perhaps volunteering.

Make safe arrangements
If he's determined, arrange for you or another adult to go, too. Plan a meeting point for if you get separated. Ask him to charge his phone fully, take a spare battery or portable charger, and leave valuables at home. Say protests should be peaceful and respectful.

In the long term

Talk about constructive debate
Talk to him about ways to express his beliefs offline and online without becoming critical or personally offensive.

Discuss being a role model
If he's campaigning, for example, about climate change, say that he should act privately, too, by living sustainably. Tell him setting a good example for peers is one of the most powerful forms of activism.

Explore group dynamics
Talk about how, if he's surrounded by peers who share his views, he may get more polarized. Explain how the truth is more important than being right, and when we take offense or throw insults, we miss out on the chance to understand other people's points of view. Discussing these values helps him develop tolerance and listening skills.

SEE RELATED TOPICS

Peer pressure and "FOMO": pp.58–59
I'm going anyway: pp.164–165

CHAPTER 3

YOUR
15 – 16
YEAR-OLD

"STOP FOLLOWING ME ON SOCIAL MEDIA."

As they get older, teens may start experimenting with their emerging sexuality by posting more revealing images on social media. Although hundreds of followers may see these shots, teens are likely to view parents' presence on their feeds as an invasion of privacy.

SCENARIO | Your teen tells you to "unfollow" her after you question a post of hers.

Your teen's social media feed is a statement of how she wants peers to see her. It's also her litmus test for how she ranks in the online "popularity contest," where the feedback, number of comments, and how quickly these appear measure attractiveness.

She may have noticed that more risqué pictures get the most attention. However, you're not her intended audience for such shots, so online comments or disapproval from you feel like an invasion of her territory.

WHAT YOU MIGHT BE THINKING

You may worry about inappropriate images being seen by potential employers or sexual predators. You may also be shocked that she's posting edgier pictures and worry she looks promiscuous.

SEE RELATED TOPICS
Social media: pp.38–39
All my friends look amazing: pp.122–123

" "

YOUR TEEN MAY FEEL THAT YOUR ONLINE COMMENTS INVADE HER TERRITORY.

WHAT SHE MIGHT BE THINKING

⊙ **She may have forgotten** you follow her if you made her accept your request when she set up her account—or thinks you don't check up on her—and is angry because she wants the freedom to be herself.

⊙ **She may spend** a lot of time getting a flattering angle for selfies and enjoy the compliments when she posts them. These comments make her feel good, so she'll resent attempts to stop her.

⊙ **Her social media image** contrasts with the one she shows you, and she may be uneasy with you seeing her more sexual persona. To maintain privacy, she may have already blocked you without you knowing from parts of her feed. She may also have secret accounts and upload her most intimate posts to sites where images disappear quickly.

HOW YOU COULD RESPOND

In the moment

Listen to her side
Ask her calmly why you should unfollow her, then explain why you feel you need to see her feed so she understands.

Discuss her image and audience
Ask her to imagine how the photo might be viewed by others. Who's her intended audience? If her profile is public, how comfortable is she with strangers seeing her images? Talk about possible repercussions. Research found that 70 percent of employers view social media profiles during the hiring process. Next time she posts a picture, can she use the "Grandma" test by asking, "Would I mind Grandma seeing this?"

Suggest a compromise
If she feels embarrassed that her peers can see she's being monitored, could you agree not to comment in public?

Accept her development
Unless her posts are more risqué than those of her peers or are being viewed by hundreds of strangers, you may need to accept that this is a phase that many teenagers go through. She may push boundaries now, but as she gradually becomes more comfortable with her identity or starts a relationship, she'll naturally want to regain her privacy.

In the long term

Show an interest
Ask her to talk you through her feed so you understand the landscape. Your nonjudgmental curiosity may encourage her to share her online life with you.

Help her feel good
If she posts more revealing selfies, she may be trying to shore up her self-esteem this way. Help her measure her worth in other ways by highlighting skills that she can feel good about.

"LET ME **SLEEP!**"

The sound of your teenager's alarm can feel like the start of a daily battle to get him out of bed. By working with his sleeping patterns and helping him get into routines, you can both enjoy a calmer start to the day.

SCENARIO | You resort to nagging to get your teen ready for school each day.

The release of the sleep-regulating hormones—cortisol, which wakes us, and melatonin, which helps us fall asleep—shifts to 2 to 3 hours later in teenagers, with melatonin release peaking around 11 p.m. Busy schedules, homework, and squeezing in time on devices also makes it harder for your teen to get the 8½ to 10 hours of sleep he needs to function well.

Research shows that if sleep deprived, your teen will find it harder to focus and remember what he's learned and may struggle to control his moods, impulses, and eating habits.

WHAT YOU MIGHT BE THINKING

You may feel angry if he was up late on his phone. As times passes, you may feel increasingly stressed, worried that he'll be grumpy when he does wake up and that he'll be in trouble at school when he's late.

❝ ❞

SLEEP DEPRIVATION HAS A RANGE OF ILL EFFECTS ON TEENS.

WHAT HE MIGHT BE THINKING

◉ **If he's sleep deprived**, he's likely to lash out and tell you to leave him alone. Exhaustion makes it harder for him to use the higher thought processes in his brain that control feelings.

◉ **If he feels nagged**, he's more likely to stay under the covers. Studies show that a nagging tone fires up the part of a teen's brain that processes negative emotions, stopping them processing words.

◉ **He may know** he'll be in trouble if late. However, his brain seeks instant reward, so he may be more interested in gaining a few more minutes in bed. Tiredness means that he's using emotion rather than logic.

◉ **If he feels you've** labeled him as lazy, he may feel he can't change your view, so there's no point trying.

HOW YOU COULD RESPOND

In the moment

Start the day affectionately
He's more likely to want to get up if you ruffle his hair, say you love him, or pour him a cup of juice.

Empathize
Give him in fantasy what you can't in reality. Say you appreciate he's tired and would love to stay in bed.

Open the curtains
Natural light stimulates the release of the hormones that wake us up. In the winter, turn the light on.

Don't take it personally
Taking his refusal as a slight will make you feel angry. Remember that lower cortisol levels in teens make it harder for him to wake up.

Remind him it's his choice
Express how you feel. Say, "I feel worried when you don't have time for breakfast. I feel it's up to you to decide whether to be late and face the consequences. I'll give you one wake-up call. If you don't have time to walk, I can't drive you to school."

In the long term

Point out the benefits of sleep
Teens are more likely to change if they understand how sleep helps them. Point out how a lack of sleep makes them short-tempered, less focused, and more likely to reach for energy drinks and junk food. Sleep is also the main time when their growth hormones are released.

Have device-free nights
Research shows that teens are often sleep deprived because they catch up on social media

at night. Make putting devices downstairs overnight a family routine and use alarm clocks.

Look at both points of view
Without blame, talk about how you want to improve mornings for you both. Swap ideas about a routine that would enable him to get 9 hours of sleep regularly.

Don't encourage long lie-ins
Late nights and weekend lie-ins disrupt body clocks more, making teens feel jet-lagged on Mondays.

◀ **SEE RELATED TOPICS** ▶
You always criticize: pp.148–149
Help! I'm already late!: pp.158–159

"I CAN'T GO OUT, MY SKIN'S TERRIBLE."

Acne affects up to 95 percent of teenagers at some point. The fact that it's so visible at a time when adolescents are particularly self-conscious can make the ordinary stresses of puberty even harder to deal with.

SCENARIO | Your teen won't go to a party because she can't hide her pimples.

Acne starts when the skin's oil glands produce more of the oily substance sebum, which keeps skin moist. Sebum feeds bacteria called *P. acnes*, which live on the skin. As these bacteria multiply, the body's defensive white blood cells block the follicles and, together with dead skin cells, form pimples.

For a long time seen as a rite of passage, acne has only recently been recognized as an actual skin disease that can have a serious impact on self-worth and mood.

WHAT YOU MIGHT BE THINKING

You may think that most teenagers have acne at some point, so she has to accept it. Depending on its severity, you may be at a loss as to how to help her feel confident facing the world.

WHAT SHE MIGHT BE THINKING

⊚ **Brain scans show teenagers** are much more concerned than adults about being judged by peers and show more signs of stress and embarrassment. Your teen may be desperate not to miss the party but may feel physically uncomfortable at the thought of others noticing her pimples.

⊚ **She may feel her skin** is out of control. She may pick at pimples to try to get rid of them. This may give her temporary satisfaction but will leave her skin looking worse, making her feel hopeless.

⊚ **Younger teens** may believe that parents should magically know how to fix their problems. She may be frustrated that any treatment you've bought isn't working and angrily accuse you of not taking her acne seriously.

⊚ **She may feel ashamed** that her skin looks dirty or unattractive. Teens are prone to catastrophic thinking, so she may believe that no one will find her attractive and worry that friends will talk about her skin behind her back.

◀ **SEE RELATED TOPICS** ▶
All my friends look amazing: pp.122–123
Anxiety and depression: pp.188–189

HOW YOU COULD RESPOND

In the moment

Empathize
Say, "It looks like your skin is upsetting you. Acne isn't your fault. Together, we can work out a treatment plan."

Explain it's nothing she's done
Acne starts deep within the skin, so make it clear it's not caused by anything she's done, such as not washing properly or touching her skin. Talk to your doctor or pharmacist about treatments. Help her get into a routine of using these morning and night.

Help her conceal her pimples
A teen's mood can lift if pimples are covered. But if she uses too much or the wrong concealer, her skin can look worse. If she's receptive, get her skin tone matched at a makeup counter and show her how to apply concealer subtly.

In the long term

Talk about squeezing pimples
Picking pimples can be a destructive habit, now recognized as a form of self-harm that can scar. Work with her to identify triggers and ask her to tell you when she wants to pick so you can distract her. Suggest strategies such as applying a face mask until the urge passes. To break harmful picking habits, ask her if she would like you to remove any mirrors and bright lights that let her inspect her skin closely and make picking more likely. Praise her for leaving her skin alone.

Go to the next level
If her skin hasn't improved after 6 months of her regime, or if she has deep acne that's scarring, see a dermatologist to discuss treatments with a higher success rate.

Don't overpromise
Make it clear that while she'll outgrow it, acne is complex and can take a long time to address. Help her keep busy and look after her whole body so her acne doesn't take on so much importance.

❝ ❞

ACNE CAN MAKE EVERYDAY ADOLESCENT STRESSES EVEN HARDER TO DEAL WITH.

"HE'S JUST A FRIEND."

Until now, your daughter probably socialized mainly with other girls. As girls and boys start to relax around one another and are less closely supervised, they're ready to break off into pairs to form more intimate relationships, but this can still feel like a big step.

SCENARIO | You notice your teen is spending lots of time messaging a boy. When you ask about him, she says that he's just a friend.

By this age, your teen may want to feel desired by a special person, and also rising levels of sex hormones may be creating feelings of sexual desire. Adolescents are also better now at reading each other and communicating mutual attraction, so dating feels easier.

Even so, her first steps toward a relationship are likely to be tentative. As boys this age can vary in how seriously they take relationships, she may want to keep any false starts private. If she does say she's considering starting a relationship, help her think about what she wants from it.

WHAT YOU MIGHT BE THINKING

You may notice she's vague about where she goes. If you suspect she has a boyfriend, you may feel sad she doesn't trust you enough to tell you.

WHAT SHE MIGHT BE THINKING

⊚ **She may feel ready** for a different type of love to the one she has had from you. She may have idealized ideas about relationships from films.

⊚ **She knows you view her** as a child, so she is likely to be self-conscious admitting this move toward adulthood. If she's going out with a boy she thinks you won't approve of, whom she doesn't really know, or who's older, she may downplay it to throw you off track.

⊚ **At the start** of teenage relationships, a couple may flirt, meet up, and be intimate. But they aren't "going out" until they've had "the Conversation." Until then, your teen may describe this phase as "just being friends."

⊚ **Girls tend to be** more into relationships, so if she has a boyfriend, this feels like a prize. She feels he's chosen her, so she's more attractive than her rivals.

SEE RELATED TOPICS
We're going out together: pp.170–171
I'm gay: pp.176–177

" "
YOUR TEEN'S FIRST STEPS TOWARD A RELATIONSHIP MAY BE TENTATIVE.

HOW YOU COULD RESPOND

In the moment

Ask about her friendship groups
If she's being evasive, ask about the dynamic among her peers. Are many dating? This will help you gauge her attitude to relationships.

Welcome male friends
Girls can find boys confusing. If she and the boy are just friends, welcome the fact that she's learning more about how boys think. Friendships with boys can also provide relief from some of the politics and rivalry in female friendships.

Ask how she knows them
If they met online, don't panic. Many teens find this an easy way to look for like-minded partners. If she wants to meet him, request this is in a public place with you nearby as a safety net. If he's older, discuss how he might be persuasive. Talk about balanced relationships and the importance of being able to say no.

In the long term

Be inclusive
Don't assume her first relationship is heterosexual. In a neutral, friendly way, try questions such as, "Are you interested in someone?"

Explore your own feelings
You may also need time to adjust to the next stage of her life. Are you bringing preconceptions from your past about teen relationships into the present?

Chat about friendship and romance
Discuss how the things that make a good friendship—trust, enjoying each other's company, having fun, and wanting the best for each other—also make healthy relationships.

Validate the fact that she's not in a relationship
If you believe they're really just friends, affirm that there's no rush. It's better to make a considered choice rather than just settle for the first likely candidate.

SEX AND CONTRACEPTION

Ultimately, it's up to your teen when they decide to have sex and with whom. But though the reality is that you have limited say, you can still inform your teen to help them make better decisions.

Though teens usually seek to keep their sex lives private, as a parent, you remain their most important source of information. While it may feel awkward at first, being brave and honest with your teen can help head off future issues, such as an unplanned pregnancy or sexually transmitted infection (STI), which can affect their future health and fertility.

1
Talk about STIs
By the age of 24, half of young people will have contracted an STI. Untreated, some such as gonorrhea and chlamydia can affect future fertility for both sexes, while others such as HIV and syphilis pose a serious health threat.

4
Discuss types of sex
For today's teens, oral and anal sex may come first. Research reveals that girls often feel oral sex is expected, while some boys ask for anal sex after seeing it in porn. Stress that all sex spreads STIs.

6
Talk about the upside
You'll be more credible if you balance any discussion of risks with talking about the importance of mutually enjoyable sex. Say that good sex is joyful and intimate, not embarrassing and painful.

WORKING THINGS OUT

8 key principles

2
Check the symptoms of STIs
Symptoms such as pain during sex or when urinating, genital changes, or discharge should be checked right away. Not all symptoms are visible, so advise regular checks. Community and college STI clinics provide confidential screening.

3
Discuss unplanned pregnancies
This will feel like a catastrophe for both girls and boys. Tell boys they bear equal responsibility for contraception. Make it clear that both genders must do their utmost to avoid pregnancy, though you would always be supportive. Also, dispel any misconceptions, such as the pull-out method being effective.

5
Recommend condoms, always
Even if teen heterosexual and male couples are using other types of protection, it's vital they also use condoms to prevent pregnancy and to stop STIs from spreading. Changes to the design mean it's a myth now that condoms reduce men's pleasure. Point out that worry-free sex is the best type.

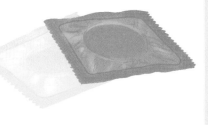

7
Bring up masturbation
Even if discussing in the third person, reassure teens that this is a natural way to learn about their bodies. Talk, too, about the effects of masturbating solely to explicit material. Studies show this makes it harder to become aroused with a real-life partner.

8
Keep talking
Say that by talking about sex, you're not giving your teen the green light, but providing information they need for their future. Research shows that when parents are open to talking about sex, teens delay intercourse and go on to have more positive experiences.

!

TAILORED ADVICE

Age by age

13–14
YEAR-OLDS

Talk about emotions
Your teen is likely to know the mechanics of sex by now. Talk about it in the context of good relationships.

Offer to answer questions
If you don't know where to begin, start by asking what your teen knows and if they have any questions.

15–16
YEAR-OLDS

Discuss emotional readiness
Help your teen consider their values and make healthy decisions about when to have sex rather than have sex to keep up with peers.

Keep an open mind
Don't assume their first romance will be heterosexual or they may find it harder to be open with you.

17–18
YEAR-OLDS

Suggest an easy test
Before your teen has sex, can they ask themselves, "Am I comfortable enough to express my sexual needs and wants with this person?"

Be assertive on condoms
Women run a higher risk of fertility issues with STIs. Due to this, it's safer to plan to have sex than to just let it happen, making it clear that condoms are a must.

"ALL MY FRIENDS DYE THEIR HAIR."

Teens want to fit in but also want to stand out and be admired by their peers. When your teen talks about changing her appearance, she may be saying she wants to try out a new identity and even leave the "old" her behind.

SCENARIO | Your teen wants to dye her hair a bright color like her friend has.

Your teen's likely to try out many identities before settling on the one she feels most comfortable with.

Dyeing her hair is a quick way to alter her appearance radically, with bold colors such as blue or pink that are hard to ignore, showing devil-may-care self-expression. This may be her way of signaling rebellion against adult authority—or marking her allegiance to a celebrity whose persona she identifies with.

WHAT YOU MIGHT BE THINKING

Dyeing hair feels grown-up, so you may mourn the end of her childhood. You may worry about what teachers and authority figures will think—and wonder why she needs to rebel. You may be concerned that she'll damage her hair.

FOR SOME TEENS, EXPERIMENTING WITH THEIR APPEARANCE HELPS THEM SETTLE ON AN IDENTITY.

WHAT SHE MIGHT BE THINKING

⊚ **She's likely to have** a strong idea of how she believes her dyed hair will look. She may believe it will be so transformative that she may risk going ahead without your permission—so it's too late for you to object.

⊚ **Dyeing her hair** may be her way of constructing a quirky identity. She may also hope it will distract from other parts of her appearance that she's less happy with.

⊚ **She may feel bored** of her normal hair color and think she'll look more grown-up.

⊚ **Changing her hair color** is her public statement that she doesn't care what adults think. Also, because it's likely to have been her idea, this signals that she chooses how she looks now.

◄ **SEE RELATED TOPICS** ►
Peer pressure and "FOMO": pp.58–59
All my friends look amazing: pp.122–123

HOW YOU COULD RESPOND

In the moment

Find out why
Thank her for telling you and talk through her reasons. Is it to model herself on a celebrity or because friends have done it? How does she think it will change her life?

Warn against permanent dyes
Explain how permanent dyes lift up the hair cuticles and damage the hair's underlying structure. Salons avoid dyeing hair for anyone under 16 because the hair is finer and the scalp is more vulnerable to damage and reactions. Hair grows ½ in (1.25 cm) a month. How long will it take to grow out if it goes wrong?

Check the school rules
Some schools have rules about brightly colored hair. Check these so she doesn't have to reverse the process instantly.

Suggest short-term options
Could she consider a vegetable-based natural dye that only coats the hair and washes out after a few weeks?

In the long term

Remember it's just hair
Hair grows out. Even if you don't like the look she's suggesting, adapt your outlook to see it as freedom of expression and view this experimentation as a normal part of her development.

Mention matching skin tone
Dyed hair is more flattering if it's within a few shades of its natural color so that it complements skin tone. Could she try an app to see what a color may look like? This may satisfy her curiosity. Or could she try a temporary dye over the holidays to see if it suits her?

Discuss others' perceptions
Adults may see bright hair colors as more rebellious. Will she mind dealing with various comments or looks?

"I NEED SOME SHAVING STUFF."

When your son says he needs to shave, it can feel like a rite of passage. Shaving is a specific response to a physical change (appearance) that has symbolic value (manliness). However, though he's starting to look like a man, he still needs your support to teach him this skill for life.

SCENARIO | After friends tease him about his facial hair, your teen asks for a razor.

On average, boys start to develop facial hair between the ages of 14 and 16. After he grows his first downy mustache, thicker hair will also grow on his cheeks, sideburns, chin, and neck. Growing enough facial hair to need to shave is the last—and most visible—marker of male puberty. So starting to need to shave may bring up complex feelings in your son about what it means to be a man.

WHAT YOU MIGHT BE THINKING

Even if expected, his request may stir up conflicting feelings, and you may feel sad about him becoming a man. Fathers feel they should be experts but may be nervous guiding sons on pitfalls such as cuts and irritated skin.

WHAT HE MIGHT BE THINKING

⊙ **Boys who are more** physically developed tend to have higher social status, so your teen may be proud and excited by this development.

⊙ **Alternatively**, he may feel embarrassed by this obvious landmark of sexual maturity, especially if friends have teased him.

⊙ **He may be worrying** about which type of razor to use, how to avoid cutting himself, and how to avoid making pimples worse.

⊙ **If he's had a difficult** relationship with an adult male, this marker of masculinity may bring up challenging feelings about what manhood means.

◄ **SEE RELATED TOPICS** ►
How tall will I get?: pp.32–33

NEEDING TO SHAVE
IS A RITE OF PASSAGE FOR
BOYS. BE THERE TO HELP
HIM MASTER THIS SKILL.

HOW YOU COULD RESPOND

In the moment

Welcome his request
Without making him feel self-conscious or teasing him, thank him for asking for your help. Say you're happy to help him find the most comfortable methods of shaving.

Offer a choice and advice
Not all boys want to go all out with a razor and shaving foam at first, or feel it's necessary. If he prefers, offer an electric shaver to start with. Help him protect his skin with gentle products that won't aggravate any acne. Tell him to shave after a shower, when the warm water has softened hair and opened pores.

Lead by example
Dads can let sons watch them shave and talk through the process. But either parent can show him how to shave in careful, short strokes in the direction of growth. Help him get into the habit of applying a good sunscreen afterward, too.

In the long term

Treat him according to his emotional age
Although he may look older, don't assume he thinks and feels like an adult.

Discuss razor care
To avoid nicks, show him how to look after blades. Rinsing them regularly and drying them will help them stay sharp and glide smoothly over his skin.

Help him space his shaves
He probably won't have to shave daily at first. Until his skin thickens with age, suggest he shaves only when needed to avoid irritating his skin.

Talk about masculinity
He may believe he has to step up to the role of being a man. Talk to him about unhealthy messages on masculinity, such as it being desirable to repress emotions and act in a dominant and aggressive way to get respect.

"I'VE GOT TO WORK OUT."

Teens who regularly exercise have been found to have higher self-esteem and a more positive outlook than those who don't. However, if your teen works out obsessively, it may cross the line into compulsive exercise.

SCENARIO | Your teen's working out the fifth time this week, after regular exercise.

Guidelines recommend at least 1 hour of moderate to vigorous physical activity daily for teens. But in a beauty-obsessed world, teens may exercise not just for health, but also to conform to ideals of how they think bodies should look, observing that such physiques can enhance social status and attract sexual interest.

Boys also often believe they need muscles and are more likely to have rigid regimes. If your teen cancels plans to fit in sessions or works out if injured or ill, encourage a more balanced approach.

WHAT YOU MIGHT BE THINKING

You may be pleased he has self-discipline but worry he's neglecting other activities and is too obsessed with his looks.

" "

REGULAR EXERCISE LEADS TO HIGHER SELF-ESTEEM, BUT EXERCISE CAN BECOME OBSESSIVE.

WHAT HE MIGHT BE THINKING

⊙ **In boys' hierarchies**, those who put on muscle mass first tend to get more social power. Your son may equate being thin with being weak. He may work out because he's in a rush to fill out and to speed up his transition from boy to man. He may also feel he's more able to protect himself.

⊙ **Your son may be competing** with friends to see who can put on the most muscle. He may think he can swap meals for protein drinks and take supplements.

⊙ **He may feel embarrassed** to talk about body image issues. He may think talking about his fears is a sign of weakness.

⊙ **The release of endorphins** during exercise may make him feel empowered and in control. The flip side is that he may feel anxious if his progress "slips."

HOW YOU COULD RESPOND

In the moment

Say it's okay to take a rest day
If he's set up an intensive regime, he may believe that he has to exercise daily. He may need to be told he's entitled to relax.

Don't accuse him of overdoing it
If you tell your teen he should work out less, he could feel criticized, become defensive, and resent your attempts to stop him.

Instead, chat after his workout. Ask if he feels his body should have a rest.

Work out his goals
If he uses apps to measure calories and exercise, ask him to explain his regime. Gauge if he's working out to be healthy or to look good. Ask what his goals are and how he'll know he's reached them.

In the long term

Encourage team sports
To take the focus off his drive for a particular body shape, suggest he tries team sports to move him toward exercise for health and social reasons.

Chat about diet
Encourage a healthy diet so that he's less likely to use unnecessary supplements. Discuss how some men use anabolic steroids, with side effects such as reducing the size of the genitalia, undermining the masculine image he's seeking.

Talk about idealized bodies
Adolescents often forget that many of the male bodies they idealize are achieved only with the use of steroids or airbrushing. Talk about how he may be chasing a body type that's impossible to obtain without risking his health.

Discuss attractiveness
Talk about while superficial looks may be noticed initially, there are many other reasons people will find him attractive.

Explore masculinity
Ask a man your son respects to question where his ideas about masculinity are coming from. Let your son know that it takes more than being muscly to be a strong man. Talk about how heroic men come in many different guises.

SEE RELATED TOPICS
I need some shaving stuff: pp.114–115

"YOU NEVER LISTEN."

Parents often feel that their teenagers don't listen to them, so it can be a surprise—and can trigger mixed emotions—when teenagers turn the tables and say that their parents aren't listening to what they're saying.

SCENARIO | As your teen lists the reasons why he should be allowed to stay out later, you're trying to deal with an urgent email.

Depending on the context, the words "You never listen" can have layers of meaning. In a dispute about rules, it can be a way for your teen to say, "I don't like the fact you're not agreeing with me." At this age, he's also pushing for you to treat him as an equal. So saying that you never listen expresses his frustration that he feels you're not respecting his views. Beyond that, he may be voicing his disappointment that you generally don't spend enough time with him or pay only partial attention to him because you're often distracted by emails or on your phone around him.

WHAT YOU MIGHT BE THINKING

You may feel defensive and hurt because you're trying your best to juggle commitments. You may also feel guilty if you're short on time or defensive if you feel you already pay him as much attention as you can.

WHAT HE MIGHT BE THINKING

⊚ **Teens tend to overgeneralize** and engage in all-or-nothing thinking. Even if you've just spent time with him, the fact that you're not paying attention now can mean that, in his mind, you "never" do.

⊚ **He knows** your basic job description as a parent includes being attentive and looking after him. Desperate to get his way and stay out late, he's prepared to say anything in the hope that by provoking your guilt, you'll cave in.

⊚ **He doesn't yet understand** the importance of keeping on top of work emails. Saying you never listen is his bid to put himself back at the top of your priority list.

⊚ **If you're often on a screen**, he may see your being busy as a sign that you don't want to spend time with him, or even as a rejection.

◀ **SEE RELATED TOPICS** ▶
Communicating with teens: pp.46–47

AS TEENAGERS GET OLDER, THEY WANT TO HAVE THEIR VIEWS RESPECTED.

HOW YOU COULD RESPOND

In the moment

Acknowledge feelings
Summarize his arguments about why he should be able to stay out late so he knows you've heard and understood.

Manage your emotions
You may feel defensive if you feel unfairly accused. If you sense your emotions boiling over, walk away. Say you'll return as soon as you can both communicate calmly.

Explain why you're distracted
If you've a pressing issue to attend to, explain this. Tell him how long it will be before he has your attention, then stick to it. Put away the phone or laptop whenever possible—these may make him feel he's less important or interesting.

Show him you want to listen
In general, don't talk over him, and answer only after a pause. Give simple acknowledgments such as "Hmm, I see" when he's speaking.

In the long term

Don't assume he needs you less
As teens get older, we tend to think they don't need as much of our time. In fact, studies show that even though parents spend less than half the time with teens than they used to, time with parents is still key for teens' well-being.

Set aside time daily
Eat dinner together or drop into his room for a chat. Linger for a minute more when you say goodnight in case he wants to talk. Take him out for lunch without expectations so he knows you enjoy spending time together.

Check how you're communicating
Do you speak more than listen? Do you often assume you know what he's going to say? Would you speak to a friend or partner like this? Many parent–teen fights are triggered by the fact that teens want parents to relate to them more respectfully. Doing so won't undermine your authority, but it will improve your communication.

SEXUALITY AND GENDER

We tend to assume that our children will remain the gender given to them at birth—either a boy or a girl. However, if your child doesn't identify with their birth gender, it's important to be supportive.

It's now recognized that gender is a spectrum, with many variations, and so is sexuality. So it's helpful for parents to think beyond binary concepts, such as "man" or "woman," "gay" or "straight."

You may need to adjust to seeing your child differently if they decide not to live as their birth gender. Appreciate their bravery and ensure that your unconditional love lets them know they are the same child to you.

1
Listen and accept
Rejecting how your teen feels about their sexuality or gender can contribute to anxiety and depression. Even if their choice is a surprise, respect their views.

4
Take time to adjust privately
If your teen identifies as a different gender, you may feel a sense of loss for the path you thought they would take. Give yourself time to adjust, and seek support if necessary.

7
Stay connected
Those who don't fit into traditional gender roles are more likely to experience social cruelty. If your child is LGBTQ+, be vigilant. Watch out for low mood, anxiety, and withdrawal.

WORKING THINGS OUT

8 key principles

2
Ask about meaning
There's a long and expanding list of how people now describe gender and sexuality. If your teen has chosen new self-defining words, ask for their personal definition. This will tell you a lot about their thinking.

3
Understand the pieces of the puzzle
Your teen has their biological sex (their sex organs at birth), their gender identity (what gender they feel), their gender expression (how feminine or masculine they want to appear), and their sexual orientation. Think of all of these as elements that add up to who they are.

5
Examine your beliefs
Where did your ideas about what it means to be a man or a woman come from? Consider how stereotypes are restrictive. Seeing how we're socialized to perform specific societal roles can help you understand their thinking.

6
Respect pronouns
Even if your teen changes their mind, it feels important to them that you respect how they want to be addressed now, whether it's "he," "she," or "they." This shows you're prepared to accept whoever they decide to be.

8
Set family values
Whoever your teen decides to be, make equality a family value. They're still your child, and your unconditional love is critical to their self-acceptance.

TAILORED ADVICE

Age by age

13–14
YEAR-OLDS

Be open-minded
Teens compare themselves a lot now and can be acutely aware of veering from gender "norms." Avoid sexual stereotyping.

Don't assume
As your teen enters the dating scene, avoid making assumptions about who they might be attracted to.

15–16
YEAR-OLDS

Don't say it's just a phase
Teens may be more open now. If your teen comes out to you, be respectful of their identity.

Keep a sense of routine
With brain rewiring and hormonal changes, all teens seek out identities now. For your child, that search may be more challenging. Make your home a safe haven where they feel understood.

17–18
YEAR-OLDS

Support self-expression
With your teen's more assured self-expression, support choices in hair, clothes, or décor.

Accept bisexuality
If your teen starts to explore feelings for more than one gender, recognize this identity as real and valid.

"ALL MY FRIENDS LOOK AMAZING."

As they become adults, teenagers want to know whether they're attractive to others. If their social media pictures don't get as many positive comments as friends' posts, they can feel worse, not better, about how they look.

SCENARIO | Your teen says she doesn't think she looks as good as her friends.

By now, teenagers know that good looks or looking cool can win status and admiration. As their sexual feelings grow, they also want to feel reassured that they're attractive enough to get a partner.

At this age, teens compare each other constantly. Research shows this comparison peaks—and confidence falls sharply in girls—at around 14 years old. Posting pictures on social media in the hope of being admired by peers makes direct comparison easy.

To compound this, teens tend toward a negativity bias, taking more notice of mean comments than compliments.

WHAT YOU MIGHT BE THINKING

You may feel that your daughter is beautiful and be frustrated that she doesn't see this. You may wonder why she compares herself to enhanced or staged images.

WHAT SHE MIGHT BE THINKING

⊚ **Even though rationally** your teenager knows that her friends' pictures have been carefully selected, airbrushed, or filtered, she'll judge herself by what she sees rather than what she knows.

⊚ **Although she may receive** lots of compliments in real life or positive feedback for her pictures, she may focus on one negative comment—or think that friends get more attention.

⊚ **If she doesn't get** as many positive comments as her friends, she may feel embarrassed about this public comparison and will delete the photos.

⊚ **You may tell her** she's beautiful, but she may think you only say this because you're her parent, not because it's true.

❝ ❞

TEENAGERS CONSTANTLY COMPARE THEMSELVES TO OTHERS ON SOCIAL MEDIA.

HOW YOU COULD RESPOND

In the moment

Listen to her concerns
Help her work out her feelings with open-ended questions. Summarize her concerns so she knows you've understood.

Give her perspective
Explain how life is about more than looks. Talk about how we all look different because of genes, lifestyles, and metabolisms. Just because someone has a different body is not a criticism of hers. Remind her of the effort peers put into making images flattering.

Help her resist negative bias
She may get online compliments, but research suggests she's more likely to dwell on images that don't get a response. Highlight this tendency and encourage her to spend just as much time appreciating compliments.

Encourage self-questioning
Suggest she notices when she's self-critical. Point out such thoughts can feed inaccurate messages—and that she can challenge them.

In the long term

Discuss social media monitoring
Studies show the more time teens spend on social media, the more they compare themselves to peers and the worse they feel about their looks. Suggest she spends less time on social media if she notices it triggering anxiety or a low mood.

Change the emphasis
Could she curate her social media and steer it to accounts for social causes or other interests that are less looks-based?

Set a good example
Make it a family value not to judge by looks. Instead, talk about what others do. Try not to talk negatively about your own appearance.

Suggest she takes a step back
Remind her that social media can leave people feeling judged. Get her to think about how it makes her feel when she doesn't receive the comments she desires. Can she pause before posting a picture to think about its message? Is it to share something exciting or to bolster her self-esteem?

◀ **SEE RELATED TOPICS** ▶
Social media: pp.38–39
Peer pressure and "FOMO": pp.58–59

"CAN I HAVE NEXT WEEK'S ALLOWANCE?"

Parents play a critical role in shaping their teenager's attitude toward money. Giving teens a fixed income to manage by themselves helps them learn the value of money and understand that it's not an unlimited resource.

SCENARIO | Your teen wants a spending cash advance to go out with friends.

Compared to adults, teens find it harder to control impulses and to resist peer pressure. Their developing brains mean they tend to favor short-term gain rather than consider longer-term consequences.

Giving your teen an allowance—and telling him he has to stick to it—is an important way to help him learn to delay gratification. Through trial and error, he'll learn to overrule impulsive, emotional thinking and make logical decisions with long-term benefits. As we move to a cashless society, with many teens receiving spending cash via prepaid cards, developing this self-discipline is even more vital.

WHAT YOU MIGHT BE THINKING

You may feel like a cash machine and irritated that he seems to engage in polite conversation only when he wants money—but you worry that if you don't give him the money, he'll be left out.

SEE RELATED TOPICS

I need a new phone: pp.30–31
Can you do it?: pp.192–193

WHAT HE MIGHT BE THINKING

◉ **Teens increasingly** eat out together. He may be desperate for extra money so he doesn't miss out on time with friends.

◉ **He may expect you** to pay up because he's grown up believing that parents have money on tap. This is because he's never earned money and you've never explained your income and expenses.

◉ **If you've ever** given him money instead of your time or given him money because you felt guilty about not giving him attention, he may equate money with love and be angry when you don't pay up.

◉ **If he takes it for granted** that you do most things for him and sort out his problems, he's more likely to assume that you'll give him extra money when he asks for it.

> A FIXED ALLOWANCE HELPS TEENAGERS TO LEARN THE VALUE OF MONEY.

HOW YOU COULD RESPOND

In the moment

Tell him to deal with the consequences
Say no. If you bail him out, he may get the message that you have unlimited money, so he doesn't need to manage his. Holding firm makes it clear that money matters.

Treat spending cash like a salary
Tell him you'll pay him a fixed allowance at the same time each week or month, like a wage. Confirm which items you'll pay for, such as basic clothing needs and food subsistence when he's out. He'll have to cover extras, such as meals with friends or nonessential clothing.

Differentiate between a want and a need
Help him prioritize spending. Suggest he works out the difference between something he needs and something that would be nice to have. He might want to meet his friends for lunch, but does he need to spend much to see them? Can he meet up with them later for ice cream or at one of their houses?

In the long term

Let him make his own mistakes
Initially, allow him to make his own choices. It's better he learns from mistakes now with small amounts of money.

Show him how to budget and think about purchases
The brain is wired for novelty, and teens are particularly impulsive. Encourage him to think about an item overnight before purchasing. Suggest a budgeting app.

Show him how to save
Research has found that savings habits improve with practice. Help him save a set amount monthly or use an account that pays interest so he learns the benefits.

Give him more control
Over time, review his pocket money so you buy less and he buys more. Make his allowance monthly, not weekly, so he learns long-term planning. Encourage earning, too. Studies found teens were more careful with money they earned.

"YOU SWEAR, WHY CAN'T I?"

It can sometimes feel that swearing is more common than it used to be. However, when it's directed at us from our own teenagers, it can lead adults to wonder where their parenting has gone wrong, and they can feel unsure how to respond.

SCENARIO | In a fight about whether your teen can go out, even though he's broken his promise to do his homework first, he swears at you.

Teens swear to feel more grown-up and to match the tough talk of their peers. If he feels his freedom is being curtailed or you're not respecting his rights, this tough talk may spill over into his arguments with you to shock you and defy your authority. If you respond by telling him not to swear—when you've used similar language in the past—he may accuse you of hypocrisy. Pointing out flaws like this helps him feel justified in moving away from your control—part of the normal process of becoming independent.

WHAT YOU MIGHT BE THINKING

Your first instinct is likely to be, "How dare you speak to me like that?" When your anger subsides, you may wonder why he thinks it's acceptable to be so disrespectful, especially if you never spoke to your parents in this way.

SEE RELATED TOPICS
Whatever!: pp.142–143
I'm going anyway: pp.164–165

WHAT HE MIGHT BE THINKING

⊙ **To your teen**, swearing may not seem as serious as it does to you because he's likely to swear with impunity on his social media feeds and when playing video games with friends. While most of the time he can filter out swearing at home, at times of high emotion, he'll find this harder to do.

⊙ **He's aware that children** aren't supposed to swear and that it's taboo, even for adults, but swearing is his way of asserting that he's now more grown-up and therefore your equal.

⊙ **If he is sleep deprived** because he's going to bed late and is on a device at night, this can make him more reactive, and it can be harder for him to regulate his emotions and how he expresses them.

⊙ **After an outburst**, he may feel guilty because his aggressive behavior is at odds with the loving relationship that usually exists between you.

HOW YOU COULD RESPOND

In the moment

Don't respond in kind
His brain is already in fight-or-flight mode, so shouting back and demanding not to be spoken to in that way will pour fuel on the fire. You'll also lose authority if you lose control.

Control your emotions
Swearing is likely to trigger an immediate stress response in you.

Take a deep breath or walk away if necessary to keep calm. Then say, "I don't appreciate being sworn at. It feels as though you need time to cool off to express yourself more clearly."

Help him be less aggressive
When emotions have calmed on both sides, ask him what he wants to say, but without swearing.

In the long term

Discuss how it makes you feel
He's still learning the full impact of how his actions make others feel. Teens tend to believe that adults are tougher and don't feel hurt as much. Say, "I feel surprised and hurt when you speak like that."

Set reasonable expectations
Explain that while he may engage in swearing with his friends, you expect him to treat everyone at home with dignity. Curtail your swearing and watch how you express anger. If you lose your

cool, discuss how you're looking at healthier ways to express yourself.

Say it stops others from listening
Discuss how while there's nothing wrong with anger, expressing it aggressively drives others away and gives them an excuse not to hear the underlying message.

Increase one-on-one time
If he swears at you a lot, it might indicate that he feels frustration at not being heard. Spend time together to rectify this.

❝ ❞

WHEN SWEARING IS DIRECTED AT PARENTS, IT CAN MAKE THEM WONDER WHERE THEIR PARENTING WENT WRONG.

"I AM STUDYING."

Procrastination is commonly used by teens to avoid the discomfort of a task they don't want to do. It can be tempting to brand teens as lazy, but often studying is put off if they feel overwhelmed, are unsure where to start, or feel they've failed before.

SCENARIO | You walk into your teen's room to find she's on her phone, not studying as she promised.

Tests are the ultimate deadlines. However, some teens deal with test stress by putting off studying for other more enjoyable activities. Wasting study time is even easier now because teens often work on computers and can be easily led off topic by the internet. Your teen is also more likely to be disturbed by social media phone notifications. At the same time, she's still in the process of developing the executive functions—high-level cognitive processes—in the prefrontal cortex of her brain. This means she doesn't have the self-discipline to delay gratification and study instead.

WHAT YOU MIGHT BE THINKING

Your worry about results can mean you constantly check on her. You may veer from thinking you're being too pushy to not pushy enough. You may catastrophize, fearing she has a poor work ethic and will never do well in life.

WHAT SHE MIGHT BE THINKING

⊚ **Your worry is contagious,** and she'll feel it, too. However, instead of feeling motivated to work, she's dealing with it by distracting herself.

⊚ **Tests evaluate a huge breadth** of knowledge, often in increasing depth. She may feel overwhelmed.

⊚ **By procrastinating,** she may be resisting your authority over her. She's asserting her independence by deciding how she spends her time. If she sees tests as irrelevant, she may also be resisting their power to define her.

⊚ **As the pressure on teens** has ramped up, she may believe you have no idea what it's like to juggle so many subjects. She may channel her anxiety into resentment toward you, lashing out if you criticize her lack of studying.

◄ **SEE RELATED TOPICS** ►
Everyone gets better grades than me:
pp.66–67

" "

TEENAGERS MAY PUT OFF STUDYING IF THEY FEEL OVERWHELMED, ARE UNSURE WHERE TO START, OR FEEL THEY'VE FAILED BEFORE.

HOW YOU COULD RESPOND

In the moment

Say you know tests are hard
Acknowledge that she has a lot to do, so she feels less defensive, and offer to help her manage her workload. Show her how to break subjects down into manageable chunks, or take them back to basics. Most teens love online videos. Calm her anxiety by helping her find "explainer" clips. She can start at an easy level and build up.

Suggest 5-minute starter sessions
When a task is daunting, often the hardest part is starting. Suggest she does just 5 minutes of studying, then takes a break if she wants, or makes just five review flash cards. The chances are good that she'll keep going.

Help her divide up studying
Suggest that once she gets started, she sets herself 25 minutes of solid work without interruption, followed by a 5-minute break. Breaking up study like this improves results because teens felt less daunted.

In the long term

Check your own experiences and expectations
Are you recalling a time when you did poorly on a test because you weren't prepared? Are you expecting too much? Parental aspiration can help children achieve, but only if realistic. Address your anxieties and expectations.

Help her develop self-control
For a day, suggest she logs her goals, what distracted her, and the outcome. This will make her aware of how she rationalizes procrastinating. Explain how every hour of studying is likely to improve her grades. Help her focus on her goals: What does she want? How can she get there?

Talk about phone use
Help her recognize how distracting phones and their notifications can be. Even if set to silent, turned off, or in airplane mode, research shows that phones can still dramatically reduce problem-solving skills. Suggest she puts it away while working.

"JUST **ONE MORE** GAME."

Teens are hardwired to take risks and will often display more aggressive and dominant behavior to establish pecking order. Video games allow your teen to do this in a virtual world, and he may often find it hard to break away.

SCENARIO | Your teen asks for time to play one more game on his game console.

While gaming may look antisocial to you, your teen believes it's a legitimate hobby that he plays with friends, which just happens to be onscreen. He's also likely to think you don't understand gaming culture if you don't recognize how important it is not to disturb a game in progress.

Nevertheless, setting limits is important. While studies show that playing video games for about an hour a day can benefit well-being, they also find that playing for over 3 hours is linked to negative outcomes, such as antisocial behavior, irritability, and poorer grades.

WHAT YOU MIGHT BE THINKING

You may be concerned that he's often irritable when you ask him to stop playing and worry that his schoolwork and fitness are being neglected. If he spends lots of time with his headphones on, glued to the screen, you may think he's isolated from the family.

▶ **SEE RELATED TOPICS** ◀

Everyone else plays this computer game: pp.94–95

66 99

GAMING MAKES YOUR TEEN FEEL IN CONTROL. TRANSITIONING BACK TO REALITY CAN BE HARD.

WHAT HE MIGHT BE THINKING

⊚ **Gaming makes him** feel competent, powerful, and in command. It's tough for him to transition back to a place that's less rewarding and where he's told what to do.

⊚ **If he plays** with multiple players, this may give him a sense of belonging and win him social status when he does well. Abruptly telling him to stop could frustrate him if he's at a vital part of the game. If he's in a team contest, it could mean letting down other players.

⊚ **He feels he deserves** this downtime and likes to immerse himself in the action to take his mind off school. It's likely he can't find anything more immediately rewarding.

⊚ **If you never play** games with him, he probably thinks you're out of touch and that you'll never understand why he loves them.

HOW YOU COULD RESPOND

In the moment

Find a natural pause
Agree that he can play until the end of the game. Recognize that it's hard for him to move on instantly after being so absorbed.

Give good reasons
Provide a reason why you'd like him to stop, whether it's so he can eat a meal, enjoy family time, or get ready for bed.

Allow transition time
Recognize he may need a few minutes to transition afterward. Try offering an incentive, such as a favorite drink, to help him make the sensory shift.

In the long term

Agree on limits
Although he may push back, he's probably seen the impact on peers who stay up late gaming and struggle at school, so he is likely to appreciate your concern. Agree on a plan and set parental controls on games so that there's less conflict over rules. Stay firm so the rules become routine.

Promote other activities
Rather than just being *against* video games, be *for* other activities. Say that he can play video games only after more important activities are done, such as sports or homework.

Suggest screen-free days
Keep consoles in common areas and have console-free days. Ask him to notice signs of overuse, such as needing to spend more time playing to feel good, struggling to stop, or falling behind on work.

Engage
Find out about the game and who he plays with. Appreciate its good points, too. For example, he's learning skills such as strategy, planning, teamwork, problem-solving, and resilience.

"I'M STAYING IN."

When your child was younger, you were in charge of party guest lists—and often most of the class got invited. As teenagers take control of social events, they can use parties to draw boundaries around friendship groups—with the result that often someone feels left out.

SCENARIO | Looking miserable, your teenager says that she hasn't been invited to a party that all her friends are attending.

We all remember the sharp pang we felt as teenagers when we didn't get asked to a party. For today's teenagers, the pain can feel even more acute because they can witness their exclusion in real time on social media. Some social media platforms have mapping options that show where friends are congregating. Beyond that, teenagers can see how the party is going as guests post pictures and videos of the event.

For teens, parties are status-building events. For one night, the host is at the top of the social tree, deciding who makes the grade. Whatever the reason your teen wasn't invited, help her put it in perspective so she can cope with her difficult feelings.

WHAT YOU MIGHT BE THINKING

If the host was previously her friend, your first reaction may be shock. You may feel angry and take it personally, feeling that you've failed if your teenager has been judged not good enough to be included.

WHAT SHE MIGHT BE THINKING

◉ **Teens are still learning** self-awareness and developing the ability to judge the effects of their actions. This "introspective ability" grows over time, but right now she may have no idea why she hasn't been invited, so will feel more confused and upset.

◉ **She may feel as though** she's in social Siberia. Even if she doesn't really like the host, she's humiliated that others can see she has been left out—both because she's not at the party, and not in the pictures.

◉ **She may worry** that secretly her other friends don't like her and that they've been talking about the event behind her back.

◉ **She may feel compelled** to check her phone, drawn to finding out which of her friends are there and look for pictures to see how it's going.

▶ **SEE RELATED TOPICS** ◀
Social media: pp.38–39
Peer pressure and "FOMO": pp.58–59

" "

TEENAGERS CAN WITNESS THEIR EXCLUSION IN REAL TIME ON SOCIAL MEDIA.

HOW YOU COULD RESPOND

In the moment

Put it in context
Ask her to think logically about why she didn't make the guest list. Perhaps there were space restrictions? You could write a list of reasons, including the most ridiculous, then rate each one's likelihood. This will help her externalize, weigh, and process worries.

Help her take her mind off it
Suggest an evening out to enjoy quality time together so she feels valued. Or could she ask another friend over who she hasn't seen for a while? Distraction has been found to be the best way to deal with fear of missing out (FOMO).

Stay calm
Don't show that you're bothered. This sends the message that it's the catastrophe she thinks it is. Help her see that we all experience social pain and recount your own experiences. Life isn't perfect, and we have to accept it's impossible to be universally liked.

In the long term

Look for a way forward
She feels rejected and as if her social life has slipped out of her control, so help her feel back in charge. Chat about how she could build a wider social circle. Or if she wasn't invited due to a fallout, does she need to think about how to repair the damage?

Watch out for hidden emotions
Even if your teen appears fine about not getting an invite, they may still be experiencing difficult feelings. If your teen doesn't want to discuss why she's staying in, find a time to talk generally about how others feel when they're left out so she can externalize her feelings.

Talk about the politics
Discuss the jockeying for status that takes place inside groups and how parties can be used to define who's in and who's out to keep cliques feeling exclusive. If she often feels on the fringes, is it time to find a new group?

TEST SUPPORT

How teenagers perform on standardized tests helps shape their futures. How they prepare, and the messages you give, can help them cope.

Whether they show it or not, your teen wants to do well on tests. However, today's adolescents tend to feel that their future success depends on the results of tests such as the SAT. If you add to the pressure, it can create anxiety that may stand in the way of them doing well rather than improve their grades. It's important to explore your motivations and whether you feel your teen doing well reflects well on you. Offering support, sharing organizational tips, and giving them confidence that they can always improve with hard work will help them keep tests in perspective.

1
Discuss a "growth" mindset
If your teen believes they're bad at a subject, encourage a growth mindset. Explain that with study and hard work, their grades will improve.

4
Talk about "good" stress
Teens tend to think that all stress is bad. Recognize their stress but explain, too, that nerves are normal when you care about something, and can be motivating.

6
Remove distractions
Recommend turning off music. Studying in silence improves retention by 60 percent. Research also shows that those who study in sight of a phone, even if not using it, do 20 percent worse on tests.

WORKING THINGS OUT

8 key principles

2
Suggest quizzes
Searching for an answer—retrieval practice—is proven to implant knowledge. Suggest online quiz sites and basing studying around past papers.

3
Manageable chunks
Breaking up study has been found to improve examination results because the brain is better at encoding information in short, repeated sessions rather than long ones. Suggest they do no more than 25 minutes' solid studying at a time. After this time, they should take a 5-minute break before starting to study again.

5
Appoint a study buddy
Being accountable to someone else has been shown to make students more likely to stick to study plans. Can your teen tell a "buddy" what they plan to cover and report back?

7
Offer perspective
Due to their limited life experience, some teens tend to catastrophize about tests. Explain that life success is based on a range of skills and that there are many ways to be smart and fulfilled.

8
Uncover motivation
For teenagers to succeed, they have to believe they're trying to get good grades for themselves, not to please parents—so goals have to be theirs. Give your teen ownership of their future rather than deciding what's best for them. Talk about what they want to do in life and how they can get there.

!

TAILORED ADVICE

Age by age

13–14
YEAR-OLDS

Develop planning skills
In the run-up to tests, help them plan ahead and set achievable goals.

Help build focus
Get your teen to set a timer and train their brain to work uninterrupted for periods of 15, 20, then 25 minutes.

15–16
YEAR-OLDS

Encourage memory tricks
Arm your teen with a set of mnemonics—patterns of associations, letters, or ideas—to help study.

Help them get started
If they feel overwhelmed, suggest they set a timer for 5 minutes, then spend just this time studying. Once they've begun, they're more likely to continue.

17–18
YEAR-OLDS

New freedoms
With fewer subjects, encourage your teen to see periods in between lessons as study periods.

Give them perspective
Help them think about *all* available options, from university to vocational courses or apprenticeships.

"GET OUT OF MY ROOM."

When your teenager shuts the door to her room, whether calmly or in anger, she's sending a clear message that she wants time alone. You may feel rebuffed or concerned, but this typical teenage behavior is seldom cause for alarm.

SCENARIO | Your teen has retreated to her room and wants to be left alone.

Your teen may need time if she's had a showdown with you or simply wants to be by herself. Whatever the trigger, teens have a real need to separate from their parents at times, which is part of the healthy preparation for becoming an adult. She's asserting her independence, and her room is her private world where she's in charge. What's more, escaping there can be an essential survival strategy. At a time when her world is changing rapidly and she has increasing social and academic demands, her room is where she can slow down and take recuperative time-out.

WHAT YOU MIGHT BE THINKING

You may be upset at her rudeness during an argument, or feel shut out and wonder how your once-affectionate child became so aloof. You may blame yourself for driving her away and feel you're a bad parent.

WHAT SHE MIGHT BE THINKING

⊙ **If she's had to accept** something she doesn't want to, disappearing into her room is the easiest way to save face.

⊙ **After a meltdown**, she's flooded with emotions and her brain is programmed to act impulsively. She needs to escape to a safe space to calm down.

⊙ **A gentle attempt** to discuss an issue can feel like an onslaught to her. Teens are super-sensitive to being "lectured," seeing this as an affront to their independence. A recent study found that parents often overestimate how supportive they seem, when in reality teens often find them overly critical.

⊙ **Her life is likely stressful**; she's dealing with homework, tests, friends, and activities. The demands can overwhelm and tire her young mind, so uninterrupted time to unwind is crucial.

SEE RELATED TOPICS
I hate you!: pp.44–45
Communicating with teens: pp.46–47

" "

TEENAGERS NEED SOME SEPARATION FROM THEIR PARENTS AS THEIR INDEPENDENCE GROWS.

HOW YOU COULD RESPOND

In the moment

Step back
Both of you cool down after a fight. When you do talk, don't lecture, as she'll want to avoid you more.

Don't insist on the last word
If she was rude, you may feel you want to teach her a lesson or not let her get away with it. But as her brain is in a state of fight-or-flight, she's no longer being rational. Talk when she's more receptive.

Phone in
A sure way to get her attention is via her phone. Text a conciliatory message. Say you're sorry she's upset and you'd love to work things out when she's ready.

Keep talking
You may feel like giving up trying to communicate, but she needs to know you're there. Your withdrawal can feel like indifference to her.

In the long term

Knock first
Respect her privacy and newly independent status by knocking and waiting for her to say "Come in" before you enter her room.

Find common ground
Time alone is important for teens, but a balance is ideal. If she rarely surfaces, entice her out with a pressure-free activity, such as going for a walk together. Talk about topics she enjoys or ask her opinion so she feels her thoughts are valued.

Troubleshoot together
Studies show that parents and teens who try to work things out have stronger relationships. Teens are learning to think in complex ways and can be ready to engage. Ask why she was upset. Explain your side, too. You may both gain insights. Also, be aware of signs that something else is going on. Changes in sleep patterns or appetite or withdrawal from social events may suggest emotional problems that she needs support with.

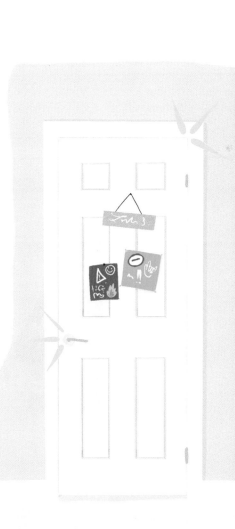

"SHE'S YOUR **FAVORITE**."

Sibling rivalry becomes a part of family life as soon as children are old enough to compete for their parents' attention. Conflict can escalate in the teen years when siblings may start to compare achievements and to define themselves in opposition to each other.

SCENARIO | When you tell your teen off for throwing a book at his older sibling, he accuses you of favoring her over him.

Teenage sibling conflict feels serious because teens are bigger, more opinionated, and likely to use stronger language. Younger siblings may resent freedoms granted to older ones, while older siblings may feel younger ones get away with more than they did at their age and may adopt a patronizing tone toward "little" brothers and sisters. Ensuring your children feel equally loved is important because if one child feels constantly less favored, this can result in lifelong resentment.

WHAT YOU MIGHT BE THINKING

You may want to deny your teen's accusation immediately. You may feel it's unfair and that he deserved the telling-off. Even if you don't have favorites, you may feel guilty, as sometimes you do prefer the child who's easier to be with.

WHAT HE MIGHT BE THINKING

⊚ **He knows that accusing you** of favoritism distracts you from the issue at hand and makes you likely to step back from telling him off.

⊚ **If both siblings** are in high school, it's easier for them to directly compare achievements academically and in areas such as music and sports, which can fuel conflict.

⊚ **If he feels his sister** is the "sporty" or "smart" one, he may assign himself another role. When you praise her, he may hear this as a criticism of himself, even though you didn't intend it to be.

⊚ **If he really believes** you prefer his sibling, he may feel that he'll never be good enough. He may direct more hostility toward her, triggering fights.

HOW YOU COULD RESPOND

In the moment

Be aware
Think about how what you do or say may be heard by a teen who's hypervigilant to signs of favoritism.

Acknowledge his feelings
Rather than defend yourself, tackle his claim of favoritism. Say, "It sounds like you think I'm being unfair because I'm talking specifically about what you did."

Hear his side
Once he's calm, ask why he lost his temper. However, as far as possible, let siblings sort it out themselves, guiding them if needed.

Be conscious
Be clear that you do your best to meet all your children's individual needs and you love each uniquely. Consider whether unconsciously you favor the "easier" child and their sibling is acting out their hurt.

In the long term

Consider sibling order
Older siblings who've helped look after younger ones in the past may feel more entitled to be bossy now, infuriating younger siblings, who want respect. Research shows that first-borns tend to identify more closely with their parents' values and can be seen as "easier" by adults. Value and listen to each child's opinions equally.

Enjoy one-on-one time
If one child often says he's treated unfairly, *is* he getting less attention? Carve out time for just the two of you and include him in some decisions so he feels

valued. Staying connected helps him process and express feelings rather than take them out on his sibling.

Encourage teamwork
Find ways for siblings to spend supportive time together without you there—perhaps taking a trip together or planning an event.

See the positives
While sibling fights sound stressful, they can help children learn to negotiate, reach compromises, and deal with conflict. When siblings resolve an issue, notice it and praise them.

SEE RELATED TOPICS
Communicating with teens: pp.46–47
You always criticize: pp.148–149

STEPFAMILIES

Being a stepparent to an adolescent with whom there is no biological bond can be difficult. For a teen who feels life is forever changed now that their divorced parent has a new partner, it's even harder.

Adolescents often keep new step-parents at a distance because the last thing they want is another adult telling them what to do. Also, however friendly stepparents are, teens are likely to believe that secretly they feel stepteens are in the way. As a defense mechanism, they may appear tough, aggressive, or withdrawn. They may also detach themselves from the family unit more quickly than they normally would.

If you're the stepparent, think carefully about your role. Stepteens are more likely to accept you if you offer yourself as a supportive, caring adult rather than as a new parent.

1
Be patient
It can take at least 2 years for stepfamilies to feel like a unit. You'll handle challenges more calmly if both you and your partner have reasonable expectations of this timescale.

4
Be on their side
Celebrate stepteens' successes, involve them in plans, and form new family traditions together. Both girls and boys report they'd rather have verbal affection, such as praise, rather than kisses and hugs from stepparents.

7
Check stepsibling rivalry
Draw up a general set of family rules so all siblings feel equal and be clear that each child is loved uniquely. Reassure your child they're as important to you as ever. Give all children a forum to express their feelings.

WORKING THINGS OUT

8 key principles

2

Stay solution-focused
Set aside regular time with your partner to work through problems. Focus on understanding your stepteen's feelings rather than complaining about behavior. Don't take normal teen behavior personally.

3

Work hard on communication
Communication in stepfamilies can falter because of the delicate relationships, leading to mounting resentments. Aim to both spend regular alone time with your teen so they feel wanted by you both. Only then, and with time, will you all feel safe enough for honest dialogue.

5

Voice stepteens' fears
Tell them you appreciate how hard it must be to see their mother or father love an adult who isn't their parent. Accept that your presence kills off any hopes they had about their parents reuniting and reassure them that if you have another child, they won't be supplanted.

6

Don't discipline
Work out family rules with the agreement of your partner, their ex, and your stepteen. Then step back into a supporting role and let the biological parents impose any discipline. Nothing causes more all-around resentment than a stepparent playing the disciplinarian role without earning the authority to do so.

8

Find shared activities
Connect with your stepteen by finding activities you enjoy doing together, such as cooking or playing a sport, ensuring these don't overlap on their natural parent's territory. Being clear that you enjoy time with them will help dissolve barriers.

TAILORED ADVICE

Age by age

13–14
YEAR-OLDS

Reassure them
Young stepteens may feel they have to look after themselves, often before they're ready. Be clear they don't have to go it alone.

Say they aren't to blame
Young teens don't get adult relationships, so may blame themselves for a split. Both parents should be clear that it was not your teen's fault.

15–16
YEAR-OLDS

Be flexible
If your teen's social life clashes with visitation times for you or your co-parent, understand their need to be with their friends.

Maintain boundaries
Teens may feel like because the original contract for their family life was broken, they can behave how they like. Uphold expectations.

17–18
YEAR-OLDS

Stay involved
Older teens may turn to alcohol, drugs, or sex to deal with feelings of rejection or pain. Don't step back now.

Impart wisdom
If teens are in a relationship, their parent could revisit issues that led to the split to help them understand.

"WHATEVER!"

While your teenager may feel grown up, he's also likely to feel frustrated that he doesn't have as much say over his life as he would like. Rather than rebel, your son may have worked out that it's easier to claim he doesn't care about your rules.

SCENARIO | When you say you'll dock your teen's allowance for being home later than promised, he says he couldn't care less.

As the most powerful person in his life, you're likely to frustrate your teen a lot. As he grows older, he wants more control over his life and feels frustrated when he doesn't get it. However, he may have realized that outright rebellion doesn't work because you're only likely to impose stricter sanctions. Instead, he may find it's safer to hide behind more neutral passive–aggressive tactics, such as ignoring you, eye-rolling, or using phrases such as "Whatever!" and "I'm fine."

Rather than take it as an affront to your authority, try to understand how he feels and help him express his feelings more directly.

WHAT YOU MIGHT BE THINKING

"Whatever!" isn't directly insulting or contradictory, so you may be confused about how to respond. You may be frustrated that he doesn't seem to respect your authority and wonder what you can do to make him follow rules.

WHAT HE MIGHT BE THINKING

⊚ **Even though** he doesn't like it, he knows that ultimately you decide the rules in the family home. Pretending that he doesn't care helps him save face, makes him feel better about his situation, and feel like he has more control.

⊚ **"Whatever!"** indicates grudging acceptance. It's his way of saying, "You may have power over me, but I'm going to pretend I don't care enough to fight about it."

⊚ **If he says** "Whatever!" when you tell him what he's done wrong, this also means, "I can't be bothered to listen." He may have observed from peers that passive resistance is a cool way to deal with authority.

⊚ **Growing up**, your teen may have gotten the message that "good" children are always obedient and never lose their tempers. He may not have learned to express his anger directly.

SEE RELATED TOPICS
It's always my fault: pp.42–43
Communicating with teens: pp.46–47

FOR YOUR TEEN, PASSIVE—AGGRESSIVE TACTICS ARE THE SAFEST WAY TO EXPRESS FRUSTRATION.

HOW YOU COULD RESPOND

In the moment

Name the problem
Tell him, "I feel you're angry and upset with me. You probably don't want your allowance to be cut, but we need to talk about my reasons, as well as how you feel."

Hear what he has to say
Let him express his point directly. This will break the impasse and open up the door to dialogue, letting him know that, rather than getting caught in an unhelpful cycle, you want to keep communication open.

Reconsider your rules
Teens are more likely to be passive—aggressive with authoritarian parents who lay down the law with comments such as "Because I said so." Research shows teens are less resistant when parents recognize they've become more responsible and let them make more of their own choices.

In the long term

Be a good role model
This kind of behavior is often learned by watching the powerful adults in their lives. Parents who use the silent treatment with children to express displeasure are more likely to raise children who use the same tactics. Model assertive, expressive communication.

Break the cycle
If he continues to use these tactics, it's likely to make you more angry over time. If you explode, he'll feel justified in not accepting your authority. Watch for rising tension and communication shutting down.

Check your criticism
If he feels repeatedly criticized or subject to unfair rules, this may be a protective distancing tactic. Do you negatively stereotype him as difficult? If he has closed down, reboot your relationship. Invite him to spend time with you and show unconditional love to help him let go of resentment.

"I'M TELLING **THE TRUTH.**"

Lying is a major conflict between parents and teens, as parents tend to put a high value on honesty. However, it helps to be aware that most adolescents tell untruths not just to mislead, but also to gain a sense of independence.

SCENARIO | Your teen says she was at a sleepover, even though her friend's mother told you they went to a party together.

Teens tell more lies than any other age group and usually far more than adults realize. Research shows that parents work out when they're being lied to only half the time. You're more likely to deal with dishonesty calmly if you see it as one of the ways she's starting to build a private life.

There are two kinds of falsehood. "Antisocial" lies are told for her own benefit, often to get herself out of trouble. "Prosocial" or "white" lies help make herself or others feel better. She may gloss over the whole truth, leave out details, or exaggerate achievements.

While not all dishonesty is serious, if she tells lies often to avoid tasks, get herself out of trouble, or look better in front of others, she'll need help to find other solutions.

WHAT YOU MIGHT BE THINKING

Uncovering a falsehood can make you question your relationship with her and your judgment. You may also feel panicky, as if you've lost control of your child because you no longer believe what she tells you.

SEE RELATED TOPICS
It's always my fault: pp.42–43
You always criticize: pp.148–149

WHAT SHE MIGHT BE THINKING

◉ **Not sharing** all the facts can be a bid for more autonomy. She wants to feel in charge.

◉ **She knows she lies** and may take pride in her ability to deceive you. In studies, at least 75 percent of teens admitted to lying on average nearly three times a day.

◉ **She may believe** dishonesty is justified if she feels you've been unfair or strict. Also, impressing peers can feel more important than being honest. Outsmarting adults can feel exciting to a teen enjoying the thrill of risk-taking.

◉ **She may keep lying** to confuse you or wear you down. She'll maintain she's telling the truth to avoid punishment. If caught, she may cry because she doesn't know what to say and is seeking sympathy or wants to divert attention from her lie.

" "

MOST ADOLESCENTS LIE NOT TO MISLEAD PARENTS, BUT TO FEEL IN CHARGE.

HOW YOU COULD RESPOND

In the moment

Make it safe to admit her mistakes
Rather than interrogate, try to connect with her. Harsh discipline is more likely to lead to more falsehoods to avoid the consequences. Talk through the reasons she lied, such as fear or peer pressure, and how she could have told the truth instead. Try not to feel that a lack of parental control has led to her falsehood. Usually, lying is part of the process of teenagers' growing independence.

Discuss the benefits of honesty
Explain that untruths are complicated and stressful to maintain and how honesty will ultimately encourage you to grant her more freedom.

Say how you feel
Teens often don't realize the effect lies have. Talk through how untruths upset and worry you because you fear you'll be less able to help if she's in a difficult situation.

In the long term

Unpack the reasons
Did she lie to avoid losing face or disappointing you? If she lied to look better, help her talk through worries so she doesn't try to cover insecurities with dishonesty. Encourage her to develop skills so she feels confident.

Avoid gender-based assumptions
Adults tend to underestimate how much girls lie and overestimate how much boys lie. Research has found girls are more likely to lie to fathers, and boys to mothers, maybe because they feel it's easier to deceive the opposite sex. Avoid labeling her as dishonest, as she'll feel it's a trait she can't change. She's less likely to lie if she feels trusted.

Be a good role model
Research shows that adults who grew up with dishonest parents are more likely to lie. Lying teaches that dishonesty rather than clear communication avoids conflict.

"I'LL WEAR WHAT **I WANT.**"

Most adolescents want to try out different identities, and their favorite way to do this is by experimenting with clothes. Your teen may dress for a subtle set of unwritten rules decided by her friendship group and be far more interested in fitting in with them than pleasing you.

SCENARIO | Your teen is going out in what you think is an inappropriate outfit.

Now that your teen decides what she wears, clothing is an easy way to express herself. Parents, though, can be confused and worried by the message. What's most likely is that she wants her outfit to be admired by her friends—and to fit in with the unwritten rules of their dress code. These rules apply to school uniforms, too. At school, girls may roll up their skirts not to attract male attention, but as a statement of how much they're willing to conform to school rules and which social group they belong to. There may be other subtle status markers that fly beneath adults' radars, such as the length of socks or how high ponytails are worn. For boys, how they wear shirts and ties is key. Try to bear in mind that most outfits are a passing phase. Soon your teen may look back at some of her more extreme choices with horror.

WHAT YOU MIGHT BE THINKING

You may be worried her outfit is too revealing and might invite unwanted attention she's not yet equipped to deal with. You're likely to judge her by your own adult set of norms and may be uncomfortable at the thought of her presenting herself sexually.

WHAT SHE MIGHT BE THINKING

◉ **Your teen is likely** to have spent time thinking about her outfit and being hard on herself for not looking "good enough." Her defiance is partly to mask her insecurity and also to assert her independence.

◉ **Your daughter** is dressing mainly for her friends and is likely to be wearing a variation of their current "uniform," which they've gleaned from celebrities and online influencers.

◉ **She's learning** that she can express herself sexually—and attract attention—through what she wears, which is both scary and exciting.

◉ **Your teen knows** that clothes give her a place in the social pecking order. Clothes—and how they're worn—are a big marker of social status for teens. Girls seen to wear the "best" style are often looked up to and copied by peers.

HOW YOU COULD RESPOND

In the moment

Tread lightly
Don't jump to criticize. This could make her feel bad about her carefully thought-through choices.

Chat about identity
Talk to her about how overly sexualized clothes can stop her from using her body fully. Discuss how stiltlike heels slow girls down and potentially cause trips and falls, while crop tops that need readjusting can make them self-conscious. Would boys put up with the same discomfort? Discuss how clothes should be a reflection of who we are and not conform to sexualized ideas of females.

Discuss her look
Ask her what she likes about her look. If it looks impractical, is there a compromise? Suggest there may be more powerful ways to reflect her style while sticking to her general image. She may not feel uncomfortable or cold now, but she may later on, so could she take a hoodie just in case?

In the long term

What's her intended message?
Discuss how the message she's sending may not be the one she intends. This isn't her fault, and no one has entitlement to her body, but she may have to deal with unwanted attention.

Pick your battles
Unless she's at real risk of hypothermia or giving offense, let her experiment. After tonight, she may want to spend the weekend in more comfortable clothes. If she's experimenting for the first time, this phase is likely to pass.

Let her comment on your outfits
Shop for clothes together and let her comment on your choices. This may make her more open to your suggestions. If she wants to show she's an individual but you still think she needs guidance, suggest a shopping trip with an aunt or favorite adult.

SEE RELATED TOPICS
Peer pressure and "FOMO": pp.58–59
All my friends dye their hair: pp.112–113

"YOU **ALWAYS CRITICIZE.**"

While it's natural for parents to want to guide teenagers, at this stage teens are particularly sensitive to criticism. If criticism becomes a feature of your relationship, it can harm your connection and damage your child's self-worth.

SCENARIO | You say your teen is behaving selfishly when he's still not ready to go out.

Teenagers need guidance, but it's important to get the balance right. Your teen is going through a stage of egocentric thinking and is less able to see your point of view. This means he tends to see criticism as you picking on him rather than you trying to improve his behavior. He also feels criticism even when there's none because teens tend to interpret facial expressions more negatively, believing we're disapproving of them, even when we're not.

As parents, we need to tread a careful line as to how we convey our wish for behavior to improve, making sure it doesn't come off as constant criticism. Criticism has been found to be the single most important factor in a child's perception of their relationship with their parent, even into adulthood. Over time, it corrodes the parent–child bond and is the most common factor in relationship breakdown.

WHAT YOU MIGHT BE THINKING

Even though you know criticism feels demoralizing, you may think it's your duty to point out where he's going wrong. If he responds rudely or goes on the counter-attack, you may feel frustrated that he isn't listening to you.

WHAT HE MIGHT BE THINKING

⊚ **Responding to your criticism** by accusing you of "always criticizing" is his way of diverting attention away from the issue.

⊚ **Even if you criticize** him only occasionally, teens are prone to "never and always" thinking. He may claim you criticize constantly and pick on him.

⊚ **If you often** do make global criticisms or ask despairing rhetorical questions, your teen may begin to feel that you don't like the person he's becoming. He may become distant to save himself the pain of disappointing you.

⊚ **Even though he won't show it**, he's likely to feel hurt if he thinks you've labeled him "selfish." He may feel he can't escape your opinion so is more likely to live up to it than try to change your mind.

SEE RELATED TOPICS
It's always my fault: pp.42–43
Communicating with teens: pp.46–47

HOW YOU COULD RESPOND

In the moment

Avoid escalating the situation
You teen is countering your criticism with his own claim that you're a bad parent in the hope that you'll respond to this instead. Resist his provocation.

Stick to the point
Rather than generalize or ask rhetorical questions, be specific about the behavior you'd like him to change and explain why.

Make gentle suggestions
If he's receptive, use "I feel" statements to describe your view. Point out how being on time helps.

Think about how he sees you
As the most powerful person in his life who knows and loves him best, he cares deeply about your opinion, even if he hides this. See his aggression as a means of defense, not as defiant rudeness.

In the long term

Encourage self-assessment
At a neutral time, ask how he can get ready more promptly. Being understanding will help him think calmly about his actions.

Break the cycle
Criticism leads teens to feel justified in their defiance and anger. If it's making you stressed and defensive around each other, it's time to reboot your relationship. Try "love-bombing." Tell him you want to spend time together, letting him choose

what you do. Make a point of not criticizing so he lets down his guard and relaxes around you again.

Talk through his feelings
Criticism is corrosive. At a calm time, ask if he really feels criticized constantly. If he does, try to notice and praise what he does right, such as setting his alarm for 10 minutes earlier. Targeted praise makes him see what he is doing right and makes him more likely to continue.

" "
OVER TIME, CRITICISM CORRODES THE PARENT–CHILD BOND.

TALKING ABOUT
PORNOGRAPHY

It's possible that, by now, your teenager has
viewed pornography, whether they came across
it accidentally, were shown it by a friend,
or looked for it to find out about sex.

Research shows that 53 percent of
11–16-year-olds have seen explicit
sexual material online, and of those,
half saw it by the age of 14. It's never
too early or too late to talk about
pornography with your teenager.
When the shock of the initial
exposure wears off, many return
to it as a how-to guide, an aid to
masturbation, or to deal with stress
and boredom.

However, the sex can be brutal, and
women are often objectified. You can
give a balanced perspective, bringing
up topics at opportune moments rather
than having an off-putting "talk."

" "

RESEARCH SHOWS
THAT 53 PERCENT
OF 11–16-YEAR-
OLDS HAVE SEEN
SEXUALLY EXPLICIT
MATERIAL ONLINE.

1

Take the indirect approach
Your teen may clam up if you
try to talk directly about sexual
feelings. Try, "I read how the
average age that a boy sees
porn is 11. That seems
young. What do you think?"

4

Discuss the human cost
Make it clear that
pornography isn't just free
entertainment. It involves
the exploitation of women
and girls who may be
underage or have
been sex trafficked.

6

Don't just talk to boys
Boys use porn more often
and deliberately, but girls
often view it, too. They can
also feel its influence in how
boys treat them and may
agree to practices they're
uncomfortable with.

WORKING THINGS OUT

8 key principles

2
Explain it's not real
According to research, 53 percent of boys and 39 percent of girls think porn portrays sex realistically. Make it clear that, just as action movies aren't about real life, porn isn't about real relationships and portrays lots of acts that aren't common.

3
Talk about its money-making aspect
Chat to your teen about how pornography is a global money-making business designed to lure in paying customers by showing the most extreme practices.

5
Talk about realism
Explain that bodies in porn are not representative. Men's penises may have been surgically enlarged, while women haveoften had all their hair removed or have undergone plastic surgery.

7
Explain its effect on the brain
Watching porn releases the feel-good chemical dopamine, followed by oxytocin and vasopressin. Talk about how studies show it can activate the same reward centers in the brain as recreational drugs and make it harder to become aroused in real relationships.

8
Be understanding
If you discover your teen has watched porn, avoid accusing, punishing, or shaming. Say you're ready to have a safe conversation about the subject so your teen understands how it can affect the body, brain, and sexual development.

TAILORED ADVICE

Age by age

13–14
YEAR-OLDS

Don't be afraid to talk
Treat porn as a health issue, like drinking or drugs, that can also trigger addiction.

Tell teens not to share
Young teens are more likely to share explicit videos because they don't understand how they shock.

15–16
YEAR-OLDS

Talk about expectations
Porn can lead some partners to push for certain acts and others to think they should give oral or anal sex. Say that sex is about mutual pleasure.

Be persistent
If boys masturbate to porn a lot, studies show they won't link sex with intimacy. Keep talking about how porn isn't real life.

17–18
YEAR-OLDS

Return to the subject
Talk about how sex isn't a performance. With the right partner, your teen can talk about what feels good for them both.

Discuss dependency
Porn viewing can escalate in college. Talk about signs of dependency, such as not being able to stop and feeling like real-life sexual encounters don't deliver.

"MY TEACHER **HATES ME**."

Teens constantly ponder questions such as, "Am I likable?", and their opinion of themselves is partly based on how authority figures treat them. If your teen feels a teacher dislikes her and treats her unfairly, she can feel hurt, angry, and powerless.

SCENARIO | Your teen explains that she got a bad homework grade because her teacher hates her.

Though questioning of authority, teens put significant store in their teachers' approval. They also have a sensitive antenna for favoritism. If your teen feels unfairly treated, she may conclude that her teacher doesn't like her. If she isn't doing well in a subject, she may claim this justifies her poor performance. It may be part of a negative feedback loop in which she doesn't try, then gets a bad grade, supporting her claim.

It's important to try to break this cycle so it doesn't impact her grades. Finding strategies to deal with unequal power dynamics can also help her learn to deal with difficult authority figures, such as bosses, throughout life.

WHAT YOU MIGHT BE THINKING

If she tends to be an under-achiever, you may think it's an excuse. If it comes out of the blue, you may feel protective and angry with the teacher but worried about sounding paranoid and worsening the situation if you intervene.

WHAT SHE MIGHT BE THINKING

◉ **Saying her teacher** hates her gives her someone other than herself to blame for her poor grades and distracts from her performance.

◉ **If she feels** unable to express her anger openly against the teacher, she may resort to passive–aggressive tactics, such as doing the minimum amount of work or eye-rolling, making any tension worse.

◉ **She tends to believe** that everything is about her, so she may not realize that it's not her personality the teacher doesn't like, but her negative attitude.

◉ **If she believes** her teacher doesn't like her and there's nothing she can do, she may develop a victim mentality, finding evidence to shore up her case and thinking there's no point in trying.

▶ **SEE RELATED TOPICS**
Everyone gets better grades than me: pp.66–67

HOW YOU COULD RESPOND

In the moment

Be supportive but fair
Bear in mind you've heard only her version, so avoid feeding into her view of herself as a victim. Be empathetic but open-minded.

Get the context
Is she basing her claim on one incident, or does she have concrete examples? Does she feel that other teachers hate her?

If so, there could be a pattern of avoidance, indicating she needs help identifying academic issues.

Remove the personal
Ask her if you can see her work to check if her teacher's comments seem fair. If you think she's not working hard, help her see that it's probably not her personality that's the problem, but her lack of effort.

In the long term

Gain perspective
Ask her to write down what happens in class, including the number of times she's criticized or praised compared with others. This objective record may help her review her opinion.

Be realistic
Explain that not everyone in life will like her. Humans subconsciously evaluate others using past experiences and prejudices against certain characteristics or even types of appearance.

Advise her to be respectful
Any dislike can be turned around if your teen shows her teacher respect and pays attention.

Promote a growth mindset
Explain that teachers respond well to pupils who give effort. Could she try harder for a month to see if the relationship improves?

Think through strategies
Suggest she asks to speak to her teacher after class. She could say she respects her authority, wants to find ways to perform better, and acknowledges any previous lack of effort. This may break the impasse and reset the relationship.

Help her see the common goal
Can she focus on the result she wants, why she wants it, and how getting along with her teacher will help her achieve it?

" "

THOUGH TEENS CAN CHALLENGE AUTHORITY FIGURES, THEY STILL TEND TO SEEK THEIR TEACHERS' APPROVAL.

"DAD SAID I COULD."

Everyone comes to parenting from a unique place because we all had different childhoods. The values you accepted or rejected from your own parents will form your parenting style. Your co-parent will have their own beliefs and priorities, so you're unlikely to agree on everything.

SCENARIO | You come home to find your teen playing video games with a friend—his dad happily watching—when he promised he'd do his homework.

You and your co-parent may have different values about what's important, how much freedom to grant teens at what age, and how to reward or punish. One parent may find it harder to say no because of insecurity, guilt, or a fear of conflict. The teenage years can also bring up stark differences in parenting approaches because more major decisions that will affect your child's future and well-being have to be made now. Studies also show that parents tend to identify more with children of their gender, so fathers may be more lenient toward sons and mothers toward daughters.

WHAT YOU MIGHT BE THINKING

You may feel intense frustration. You may think your partner should know better and be angry at him because you feel he's made your job harder. You may be annoyed with your teen for exploiting your differences to get his way.

WHAT HE MIGHT BE THINKING

⊚ **Your teen is likely** to have worked out your partner is the softer touch and is prepared to use that to get what he wants.

⊚ **After a long school day**, he just wants to relax with a video game. The instant gratification of doing what he wants feels good—even though he had promised to do his homework and he knows it could land both him and his dad in trouble.

⊚ **He may see your differences** as a chance to play you off against each other. They're a useful distraction from his behavior, and he sees the confusion as a chance to bend the rules.

⊚ **If you disagree** in front of him, he could lose respect for both of you because you both lose authority when you challenge each other.

◀ **SEE RELATED TOPICS** ▶
Communicating with teens: pp.46–47
Just one more game: pp.130–131

HOW YOU COULD RESPOND

In the moment

Discuss your views in private
Avoid showing disapproval of your co-parent's decisions and undermining them in front of your teen. Instead, agree you'll talk about your different thoughts together later.

Avoid being pushed into a difficult decision
If your teen asks you to agree to something and you feel you need more time to confer with your co-parent, say clearly, "I need to talk to your mother/father first."

Make it clear your decisions are joint
Even if you both have different views, let your teen know you were both involved in what you've decided now. Make sure he hears this message, saying, "We've both decided it's time you stopped playing your video game now and started your homework."

In the long term

Talk through your values with your partner
Discuss why you differ in approach. How were you disciplined as teenagers, how much freedom did you have, what were your parents' expectations of you, how did they express affection, and what was their attitude to possessions? Draw up agreed rules on conflicts such as phones, bedtime, spending cash, and video-game use.

Reframe your differences
See differences as a benefit. Parenting is about teamwork, which needs different strengths. You're likely to see a quick improvement in your teen's behavior and tendency to oppose you both once you put on a united front. If you're separated, behave like business partners. Business partners don't have to be friends, but they prioritize the successful launch of their project—in this case, your teenager. That's most likely to happen if your teen isn't caught in the middle of your differences.

"I DON'T KNOW HOW THOSE CIGARETTES GOT INTO MY BAG."

Despite public health campaigns that have helped cut smoking rates, teenagers still experiment with smoking. If you can help your teen understand why she's drawn to try cigarettes and to foresee how much smoking can affect her life, she may make better decisions.

SCENARIO | You see a half-empty pack of cigarettes in your teen's bag.

As her independence grows, your teen is wired not only to seek new sensations, but also to want to fit in with peers. However, the part of the brain that averts risky behavior—the prefrontal cortex—isn't fully developed until her mid-twenties.

Even when she knows the risks, the thrill of breaking rules, looking grown-up in front of peers, and the chemical buzz from cigarettes can be hard to resist. Informing her about the long-term impact of smoking and how quickly she can get addicted is key. Studies show nicotine disturbs the adolescent brain's rewiring, so teens get hooked quickly. Also, the earlier smoking starts, the harder it is to stop. Nine out of 10 adult smokers started in their teens.

WHAT YOU MIGHT BE THINKING

You may be shocked that despite the health warnings and cost, she's been so irresponsible. You'll wonder if peer pressure was a factor and if she's addicted. If unexpected, you may think you don't know her. You may consider withholding money from her.

> " POINTING OUT THE EFFECTS OF SMOKING CAN HELP TEENS MAKE BETTER DECISIONS.

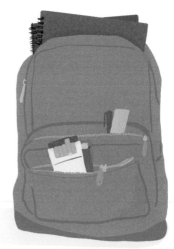

WHAT SHE MIGHT BE THINKING

◉ **Even if you've caught** her red-handed, she's likely to deny the cigarettes are hers and may claim that she has no idea where they came from or that a friend put them there. Though she knows this sounds implausible, by planting this seed of doubt, she hopes you'll hold back on punishment.

◉ **Even though teens know** smoking causes cancer, it's something exciting and forbidden to do with friends. Fitting in with peers feels more important.

◉ **She may believe** she can give up at any time because she doesn't realize that even light smoking leads to addiction.

◉ **If she's in the early days** of addiction, she may feel smoking temporarily relaxes her. She may have moved from vaping to cigarettes because they feel more grown-up.

SEE RELATED TOPICS
I'm telling the truth: pp.144–145
Vaping isn't bad for you: pp.208–209

HOW YOU COULD RESPOND

In the moment

Get her perspective
Be curious rather than lecture. If she says they're not hers, ask what she thinks about smoking and how many of her friends smoke. This may reveal her attitude to smoking, and you can give her more information.

Tell her addiction is rapid
Studies show that nicotine addiction can take hold within days. She may think she's experimenting, but more than a third of teens who try a cigarette smoke daily before leaving school.

Talk about its immediate effects
Teens feel indestructible and are motivated by immediate, not long-term, outcomes. Focus on the downsides now. She may know it causes cancer but not that it harms the developing brain. Research shows nicotine lowers IQ in teens and affects focus. They also get bad breath and waste money.

Keep talking
Say you're there to help her quit if needed. If she admits she wants help, discuss how to avoid trigger situations and help her find other ways to de-stress.

In the long term

Ask older peers to talk to her
Almost all young adults who smoke say they bitterly regret starting. Ask a friend or cousin in this age group who she admires to tell her how it took hold in their life and its effects.

Explore how to say no
It's hard for teens to stand up to peers. Talk through scripts she can use without losing face—perhaps a firm, "No, I don't smoke." She could distract friends to do something else or say she finds it too upsetting because a relative died from a smoking-related illness.

Set boundaries
Say you don't want to fund her smoking, so if she continues, half of her spending cash will go into a savings account. This leaves her some money and autonomy but not enough to buy many cigarettes.

Say how smoking takes over
Teens want to be independent but fall into the hands of the tobacco industry when they smoke and sacrifice their health for profits.

Set a good example
If you smoke, try to quit. Talk about why you're glad to do so.

"HELP! I'M ALREADY LATE!"

By this age, teens have many demands on their time. Combined with the fact your teen's body clock is set to a later schedule and his brain is still developing skills to plan ahead, it's likely that he'll have plenty of last-minute panics.

SCENARIO | Your teen asks for a ride to school because he got up too late to walk.

Until now, you probably organized much of your teen's time and took him to where he needed to be. Now, more of this responsibility falls to him, but the parts of his brain that govern planning ahead and help him foresee the consequences of being late are still connecting.

The other key reason he may often be running late, especially in the mornings, is that the release of the wake-up hormone cortisol and the hormone melatonin, which helps trigger sleep, varies by 2 to 3 hours in teens. That means he genuinely finds it harder to get up on time.

WHAT YOU MIGHT BE THINKING

You may feel annoyed if he's been going to bed late and/or hasn't had the self-discipline to get up on time. You may also worry he'll get into trouble or that his lateness will reflect badly on you.

WHAT HE MIGHT BE THINKING

⊙ **To get something done**, he may feel he needs an adrenaline surge and pressure. He may also believe that, just because he once got up and out within 10 minutes, he can always pull this off.

⊙ **If he's overloaded** with work and activities, he may get a larger-than-normal surge of the stress hormone cortisol—which wakes us—when he opens his eyes each day. Remembering everything he has to do may make him unfocused and panicky. If he's anxious about school, he may be trying to put off going in.

⊙ **Because the brain's executive functions**—which govern responsible decision-making—are still developing in his frontal lobe, he may prefer the gratification of staying in bed for a few extra minutes, even if it's more stressful afterward.

SEE RELATED TOPICS
Let me sleep!: pp.104–105
Can you do it?: pp.192–193

" "

TEENS' REDUCED CAPACITY TO PLAN AHEAD CAN MAKE KEEPING TRACK OF TIME A CHALLENGE.

HOW YOU COULD RESPOND

In the moment

Stop coming to the rescue
You may help him today, but say that later you'd like to brainstorm ways he can be on time, such as getting up 15 minutes earlier. Say from now on, you won't drive him, so he'll have to face the consequences of being late. Stick to your guns—you're teaching him the lifelong skill of punctuality.

Uncover his reasons
That day, talk to him about patterns. Is he late to everything, or just for some things he dislikes? Is he getting up late because he's worried about school, or so you have to drive him? Helping him understand his reasons can help him address the issue.

Focus on the positives
Notice and comment positively when he's prompt so he feels a sense of mastery. Help him recognize how much more relaxed he feels when he's not constantly rushing.

In the long term

Take a fresh look
Together, analyze how much time each morning task takes. Suggest he adjusts his getting-up time accordingly. He could try a step-by-step approach. First, he could stop hitting the alarm snooze button. Next, he could set the alarm 5, 10, and then 15 minutes earlier each morning. A time-management app may also help.

Discuss priorities
Explain that while all teens have roughly the same number of after-school hours, it's his choice about how he uses them. Help him break down time into manageable blocks and ask if he needs to cut down on activities so he gets to bed earlier.

Give him a watch
Using his phone as a watch could distract him. Wearing an analog watch will help him visualize and register the passing of time.

"MY LIFE IS OVER IF I DON'T GET THESE GRADES."

We live in a world that measures success by increasingly narrow standards. As early as elementary school, children start to understand that they need the best test results to get into the best colleges so they can land the best jobs and be successful in life.

SCENARIO | Your teenager is anxious because she's pinning all her hopes on getting high grades on her standardized tests.

If your teen works hard and has been told to aim high, she may have observed how much approval she gets from adults for her achievements. She may believe that much of her value as a person is tied up in academic success. Because adolescents are prone to either-or thinking and don't have the perspective to know that there are many ways to be successful, she may be panicking that she won't be able to live up to expectations. Girls are more likely than boys to tie self-worth to the external validation of test results. So not only is she holding herself up to these high standards, she's also criticizing herself if she falls below them, and may catastrophize if she falls short.

WHAT YOU MIGHT BE THINKING

On the one hand, you may be eager for her to get high grades to optimize her opportunities. But at the same time, you may worry she's putting so much pressure on herself that she won't be able to cope with tests.

" "

TEENAGERS ARE PRONE TO EITHER-OR THINKING AND CAN FEEL THE WEIGHT OF EXPECTATION.

WHAT SHE MIGHT BE THINKING

⊙ **She may be so shaped** by others' expectations that she can no longer express feelings for fear of letting others down. But bottling up emotions can lead her to bury them, and they may resurface as issues such as depression, anxiety, or self-harm.

⊙ **She may feel** that everyone else is smarter than she is and that she'll be found out.

⊙ **If she's a perfectionist**, she may focus on the grades she didn't get, even if she got a high score. She may also find that working even harder is the one way to ease anxiety, which leads her to turn in only work of an extremely high standard. When she gets positive reinforcement, this reinforces her fear of failure.

HOW YOU COULD RESPOND

In the moment

Don't say she's pressuring herself
This sounds like it's her fault when she's likely to be feeling pressure due to a range of factors, from others' expectations to cultural messages about success.

Help her manage expectations
Expectations are powerful. They can motivate but also cause stress. Suggest she sees pre-exam tests as a constructive guide to what she needs to work on. Help her see that life has ups and downs. Can she draw a pie chart showing what's in her control (such as how much she studies) and what's outside of her control (such as the questions)? This prepares her for uncertainty.

Help her challenge her thinking
Explain that perfectionism triggers anxiety, hampering clear thinking. Help her move toward expecting progress, not never expecting to fail. If she hears "must" and "should" in her mind, suggest she replaces these with more helpful, compassionate words such as "try," "attempt," and "perhaps."

In the long term

Talk about different paths
Ask her what she really wants rather than what she feels she's expected to do. Listen without judgment, and whatever path she's considering, explore the many ways to reach this goal.

Talk about what measures worth
Remind her that tests don't give grades for character, persistence, or creativity—and that it's now recognized that there are eight types of intelligence, most of which aren't measured by academic tests.

Watch your words
You may say you just want her to be happy, but is she hearing, "We want you to be happy as long as you don't disappoint us"? Are you secretly hoping she'll do well to reflect well on you? Unpack these feelings, as she'll register them.

Share your mistakes
Tell her when you didn't achieve what you aimed for and how you found other routes to reach your goal. Talk about the benefits of not always getting what you want.

SEE RELATED TOPICS
Everyone gets better grades than me: pp.66–67
Test support: pp.134–135

EATING ISSUES

Every teen has different eating habits, which can vary throughout adolescence. Many go through phases of picky or disordered eating, but a small number will develop an eating disorder.

Half of adolescent girls and a quarter of boys say they're trying to lose weight. For some, eating issues may develop if their focus on what they eat takes over their lives.

How your teen eats may become a way to express anger or a form of self-harm to deal with the negative feelings of not being good enough.

Eating can also be your teen's way to feel in control when under stress—for example, before tests. Disorders such as anorexia, when someone eats very little, or binge-eating, when large amounts are eaten secretly, are visible. Others, such as bulimia, where a person induces vomiting after eating, are less evident if their weight doesn't change.

CONTROLLING THEIR EATING CAN BE A WAY FOR TEENS TO MANAGE OTHER AREAS OF THEIR LIVES.

1
Allow for negative feelings
Eating issues occur more when teens feel they shouldn't voice negative feelings. Let them speak openly, even if their feelings are hard to hear.

4
Break the silence
To help them open up, at a calm time, ask, "What's worrying you?" Check if their concerns may be affecting areas such as eating, as well as sleep and schoolwork.

6
Avoid self-criticism
Teens are more likely to be unhappy with their weight if they see the adults in their lives criticizing their bodies.

8
Understand the conflict
Your teen has a mental tug of war. Food is their enemy, so eating may add to feelings of worthlessness, but they also crave food.

WORKING THINGS OUT

10 key principles

2

Be alert to the signs
Teens with eating disorders are more secretive about food, may want to eat alone, hoard food, or may express shame or guilt about eating.

3

Eat together
If you're worried, don't set your teen apart by giving them special meals or portions. Take a whole-family approach, eating together and focusing on the conversation rather than the food.

5

Be prepared for anger
Suggesting changes to eating will make your teen fear you're removing their coping strategy. Say you're there when they want to talk. It's likely to be a huge relief for them when they do.

7

Avoid nagging
Don't nag your teen about eating or demonize certain foods. This gives the issue of food too much power, and your teen may rebel. Rather than talking about "good" and "bad" foods, try referring to "whenever" and "occasional" foods.

9

Look after yourself
You may wonder if you're to blame. You might also swing from relief when your teen's eating seems be more balanced to despair when you see a setback. Seek help if you need it.

10

Be a good role model
Make sure that you model healthy eating behavior. Avoid constantly counting calories and instead place the emphasis on eating a healthy, balanced diet and allowing for the odd treat.

TAILORED ADVICE

Age by age

13–14
YEAR-OLDS

Understand development
In puberty, girls put on about 20 percent of their body weight. Reassure girls this is a natural part of growing up.

Build awareness
Snacking becomes part of the way teens bond now. Help your teen notice their body's "full" cues.

15–16
YEAR-OLDS

Discuss body types
Talk about how our genes help determine our body type and how a healthy weight varies for each person based on build.

Discuss other effects
Teens still compare looks a lot now. Point out that disordered eating can cause tooth decay; bad breath; and dry, flaky, uneven skin.

17–18
YEAR-OLDS

Look at cultural messages
Your teen can analyze their own thinking, so question unhealthy messages that may lead to self-criticism.

Suggest help
In cases of compulsive overeating, suggest they attend some Overeaters Anonymous (OA) meetings to get support for emotionally sober eating.

"I'M GOING ANYWAY."

Now that your teenager is getting older, he wants to have more control over his social life. Because he's so scared of missing out on fun with his friends, he may try to defy you if you attempt to thwart his social plans, no matter what your reasons are.

SCENARIO | You tell your teen he can't go a party because it's too far away.

Every parent hopes their child will abide by their rules. The likelihood, however, is that your teen has disobeyed you—you just didn't know about it. Rather than provoke a confrontation, which is hard work or brings the risk of you clamping down on his social life, your teen will generally find it easier to lie about where he's been and what he got up to. However, if he has to tell the truth for logistical reasons, and you try to stop him, he may threaten to go anyway. Because he feels so frustrated by your refusal, putting on a show of bravado makes it appear that he's more powerful than he is.

WHAT YOU MIGHT BE THINKING

His threat to disobey you is likely to make you feel shocked and disappointed, and you may worry that he no longer respects your authority. You may be scared he's getting out of control and wonder if you should be stricter.

WHAT HE MIGHT BE THINKING

◉ **As he gets older**, your teen knows that you'll find it difficult to stop him from leaving the house. However, he's worried about losing your love and approval, too.

◉ **In the moment**, when he's arguing with you, he's testing the boundaries and how far you're willing to go to stop him. Despite his bravado, standing up to you like this feels very scary and uncomfortable for him.

◉ **If all of his friends** are going, being there is important to his social status. He'll build up the event and its importance. To your teen, being there can feel like a matter of life and death.

◉ **He'll feel** that you're being unfair and unreasonable and will claim that everyone else's parents are letting them go.

SEE RELATED TOPICS
Peer pressure and "FOMO": pp.58–59
Whatever!: pp.142–143

HOW YOU COULD RESPOND

In the moment

Don't be afraid of his anger
Your teen may use his anger to try to get you to back down because you can't face a fight. If he shouts, say you'll resume the conversation when he can communicate calmly.

Explain your perspective
He's likely to feel immune to risk. Be clear that you're not trying to control him, but your priority is to ensure he's safe. Ask for details. If he claims that all his friends are going, say you'll check with their parents. Will there be adults present and how will he get home? If he's exaggerated or not told the truth, he's liable to back down.

Show an interest
Is there a girl going who he likes? Does the invite give him admission to a new social crowd? Understand his peer group are his new group and it feels vital to belong.

State the consequences
Say that though you don't expect to need to, if he sneaks out, you'll follow through with consequences, such as assigning extra chores.

Look for a compromise
Is there a way he can go but you get peace of mind? Can he take a taxi or ride-share service, carpool, or let you track his journey home?

In the long term

Focus on other activities
Generally, he'll deal with "fear of missing out," or FOMO, better if he shifts his attention to other enjoyable activities, such as having another friend over or watching a movie with you if he can't go out.

Avoid a power struggle
As he gets older, think of yourself less as an air traffic controller, telling him what to do, and more

as a life coach, helping him to make better decisions. Over time, your values and concerns will become his internal conscience.

Keep a strong connection
You'll be more influential if you invest one-to-one time with him, being clear you enjoy his company. Avoid constant criticism, too, which can be corrosive. Give five positive comments for each negative one.

❝ ❞

YOUR TEEN'S PEERS ARE HIS NEW GROUP, AND IT FEELS VITAL TO HIM TO BELONG.

"I DON'T HAVE TIME."

As your teen moves toward independence, she may feel that she should decide how to use her time, especially if she believes she has enough on her plate already with homework, extracurricular activities, and keeping up with friends. A request for help from you can feel like just one more task.

SCENARIO | When asked, your teen says she doesn't have time to fold the laundry.

As part of the process of separating from you, your teen puts her needs first. She's unlikely to see your perspective—that you need help with housework—and instead feel that you're trying to control her or stop her from doing activities she enjoys. Her need for instant reward, coupled with the fact she finds it harder to foresee consequences, means that housework can feel boring and unnecessary. Even so, it's worth persevering. Helping out around the house will make her feel like part of a family team. Giving her regular tasks will also help her develop a sense of responsibility, plan her time better, develop a "pitch-in" attitude, and learn important life skills.

WHAT YOU MIGHT BE THINKING

You may be annoyed that despite all you do, she won't help, but also worry that chores aren't the best use of her time if she has a lot of schoolwork to do.

" "
TO YOUR TEEN, A HOUSEHOLD CHORE FEELS LIKE ONE MORE THING ON THE LIST ADULTS TELL HER TO DO.

WHAT SHE MIGHT BE THINKING

● **While you believe** you're giving her adult responsibilities, she's likely to view your request as treating her like a child.

● **Because teens** tend to be self-centered, she may believe that if she has to help, she should have to fold and put away only her *own* laundry.

● **Your teen may think** that if she agrees, it will set a precedent, and household tasks might impinge on other activities she prefers.

● **As part of gradually** getting ready to leave home, your teen may think that she won't be living with you forever and believe her "job" is just to do schoolwork. She's likely to believe it's a parent's job to run the household.

HOW YOU COULD RESPOND

In the moment

Calmly ask why she can't help
She's likely to be thinking about her own needs, so explain your viewpoint and how it would help you.

Be specific
Show her how a task should be done, as she may be avoiding it if she's unsure about how to do it correctly. Point out how little time it should take if she focuses. This helps her visualize doing it, which in turn makes it easier to start.

Agree on a realistic deadline
Expecting her to drop everything immediately is likely to trigger resistance. Negotiate a deadline.

Promote willing teamwork
Make it clear that everyone should pitch in to make home a nicer place to live, and allocate age-appropriate duties fairly to all children. Don't pay unless she's going beyond the call of duty, as it sends a message that you need to bribe her to do a job she should do anyway.

In the long term

Praise, don't nag
Notice when she performs a chore well so she's more likely to want to repeat it. Studies show that when teens hear critical, negative, or pressuring requests—especially from moms—it fires up the emotional, reactive part of their brains, and they tune out. Instead, researchers say parents get better results by using encouraging tones. Or use no words at all. To avoid accusations of nagging, instead text her a picture of the unfolded laundry pile with a funny emoji.

Say she's ready for responsibility
To counter claims that you're treating her like a child, say that now she's older, you know she'll do a good job. This positive reframing helps her feel able and willing.

Hold a family meeting
Agree on a chores "plan" and pin it up somewhere visible. Having a say in how and when she helps will make her more likely to cooperate. Being clear that you all have to stick to it will help her feel like an equal with a stake in the family business.

SEE RELATED TOPICS
I'll clean my room in a minute: pp.28–29
Can you do it?: pp.192–193

"I DON'T FEEL SAFE
AT SCHOOL."

In recent years, schools have no longer felt as safe as they once did, and 24/7 news cycles with repeated footage of violent events can increase the perception of a threat. If your teenager feels in danger at school, this adds to the anxieties of the teenage years.

SCENARIO | When you both see a headline about a violent incident at another school, your teen says he worries about his safety at school.

Images of school violence can bring up many conflicting emotions in teens. Adolescents already create a "personal fable" that tells them they're special and immune from threats that harm others. They also have a fundamental belief in fairness and know it's unfair when young people are killed.

However, these feelings can be disrupted by the knowledge that sometimes schools are attacked.

Repeated images showing the aftermath of violent events, as well as a rising trend in lockdown drills in schools, may leave your teen feeling increasingly anxious.

WHAT YOU MIGHT BE THINKING

Anxiety about sending him to a place that could be randomly attacked can mean you struggle for the right words. You may want to reassure him but also prepare him.

WHAT HE MIGHT BE THINKING

⊙ **Your teen may be angry** that, as well as worrying about grades and friendships, he's living in the kind of world where he also worries about being physically safe at school.

⊙ **He may be frustrated** that, despite adults' undertakings to make schools safer, nothing seems to have changed.

⊙ **He may worry** about what he would do if an intruder entered his school. While a practice drill may help him think this through, it may also make the threat feel more serious, and he may be cynical that safety drills will protect him.

⊙ **He may become hypervigilant** to alarms, loud noises, and sudden shouting and struggle to focus.

◀ **SEE RELATED TOPICS** ▶
Social media: pp.38–39
Anxiety and depression: pp.188–189

ROLLING NEWS
COVERAGE CAN
DISTORT YOUR TEEN'S
PERCEPTION OF THE
LEVEL OF A THREAT.

HOW YOU COULD RESPOND

In the moment

Thank him for telling you
Boys in particular may feel embarrassed to admit fear, thinking they should be tough. Asking him about how he feels and what he's afraid of will help alleviate his anxiety.

Offer calming statements
Suggest he writes mantras such as "Chill" or "Let it go" discreetly on his pencil case or in a notebook to look at if he feels anxious in class.

Refocus his attention
In news reports on incidents, point out the helpers to show there are always good people ready to step in.

Encourage him to share his thoughts with friends
He knows that only his friends understand. Confiding in them, and even joking with them, will relieve his stress.

In the long term

Help him make a difference
At this age, he'll start to develop strong opinions about how to make his school safer. Encourage him to stand up for his safety by volunteering for the student council or arranging a meeting with the principal to discuss safety.

Point out the effects of social media
Seeing replays of violent incidents can cause secondary trauma, with images staying in the memory longer. Talk about how the more he watches, the more his mind is tricked into thinking something bad is likely to happen.

Discuss ways to feel more empowered
Encourage your teen to find ways to stand up for himself, whether it's taking up martial arts or joining a debate club where he can learn how to articulate his concerns and views.

"WE'RE **GOING OUT** TOGETHER."

Your teen's first relationship is an important part of his development toward adulthood. Telling you about it is a big step. You may be pleased for him, but also wonder about how the bond will develop and how to help him handle this new stage in his life.

SCENARIO | When you ask your teen if he's spending the evening with his friends, he replies that he's actually going out with his girlfriend.

Your teen will bring all he's learned from watching and interacting with you to his new relationship. He'll also discover how to negotiate intimacy and learn more about how his actions affect others.

If your teen tends to hide his emotions, having a partner he can confide in can open the floodgates, letting him express himself in ways he couldn't before. This first relationship will also influence how he views future ones, so it's important to take it seriously.

WHAT YOU MIGHT BE THINKING

While you knew it would happen, you may still feel unprepared. You may be unsure of your role and whether you should have new house rules. You may think that if they're going public, they may already be having sex.

" "

YOUR TEEN'S FIRST RELATIONSHIP IS A MOVE TOWARD ADULTHOOD AND INDEPENDENCE.

WHAT HE MIGHT BE THINKING

◉ **Being in love** takes getting used to. He'll be experiencing lots of highs and lows. Research shows that newly-in-love teens are prone to "hypomania"—a mood state in which they quickly change from euphoria to despair. Also, it was found that they had better moods in the mornings and evenings, slept for shorter times but more deeply, and had improved concentration.

◉ **Being in a relationship** is a big step toward building an independent life, away from family. As part of this separation, he'll want to keep many details private.

◉ **Going public** is a major commitment. He knows he's likely to be the target of gossip at school, resentment from his friends, and that you may be curious about whether he's having sex.

◀ **SEE RELATED TOPICS** ▶
Can my boyfriend sleep over?: pp.194–195
Consent: pp.196–197

HOW YOU COULD RESPOND

In the moment

Be supportive
It may be hard to take his relationship seriously because relatively few first loves last, but avoid minimizing his feelings as puppy love. To him, they're real.

See the positives
Being in a mutually caring relationship means that your teenager is probably avoiding the casual sex that some peers may be engaging in.

In the long term

Discuss ground rules
Welcome his girlfriend but talk about boundaries, such as how much time they spend in his room and whether his door is shut.

Talk about real relationships
Talk about what loving, mutual, equal relationships look like; the importance of emotional (as well as physical) intimacy; and the difference between lust and love. Explain that there's no place for emotional or physical abuse in relationships. Signs he's in a healthy one are being confident and relaxed, taking responsibility, and balancing his romance with his friends and interests. In a bad relationship, he may lose confidence, show unexplained anger and sadness, and feel pressured and controlled.

Suggest boundaries and balance
Research shows 85 percent of dating teens expect to hear from their partner at least every few hours. Suggest he tries to find a balance with his girlfriend before problems surface and his work suffers.

Help him communicate
He may have an idealized view of relationships and panic when he hits a rough spot. Talk through the importance of honesty and how different opinions aren't always bad so he learns to resolve issues.

"I HAVEN'T TOUCHED THE RUM."

To a teenager, alcohol is a way to have fun with friends, look more grown-up, and feel confident. Teens tend to believe the effects of alcohol fade once they're sober, but a growing number of studies have found a range of long-lasting and wide-ranging effects on the adolescent brain.

SCENARIO | When you go to pour yourself a drink, you find the bottle is half-empty.

Alcohol is known to lower inhibitions and encourage risky behavior. Your teen may see it as a way to bond with friends, but she should know the risks. As well as the possibility of alcohol poisoning, it can have lasting effects on her concentration, memory, and learning ability. Drinking also makes her more vulnerable, for example, to assault or having an accident. You may see drinking as a rite of passage, but stress that the longer she waits, the safer she'll be.

WHAT YOU MIGHT BE THINKING

You may assume that you would be able to tell if your teen has started drinking and not want to believe she's lied to you. If the evidence is clear, you may worry that you don't know what she gets up to with friends.

WHAT SHE MIGHT BE THINKING

◉ **Your teen** has probably seen you drink with no obvious bad effects, so she may assume that it won't harm her either.

◉ **She may hate** how alcohol tastes—particularly as her taste buds are more sensitive to bitter flavors—but wants to keep up with friends anyway and may like the way alcohol makes her feel more relaxed.

◉ **When she starts drinking**, she may falsely believe that being "wasted" is an excuse for behaving irresponsibly.

◉ **Even if she realizes** that you know she drank the rum, she's likely to keep denying this because she's ashamed of her deception and worried about your punishment.

◄ SEE RELATED TOPICS ►
It's always my fault: pp.42–43
I'm telling the truth: pp.144–145

STUDIES SHOW THAT ALCOHOL HAS LONG-LASTING EFFECTS ON THE TEENAGE BRAIN.

HOW YOU COULD RESPOND

In the moment

Don't turn a blind eye
Ask your teen directly if she and her friends drank the rum. Say you won't punish her for telling the truth and that teenage alcohol use is an important issue to talk about.

Talk about how alcohol acts differently on teens' brains
If you launch into a lecture on the dangers of drinking, your teen is likely to get defensive, thinking you're suggesting she has a drinking problem. Instead, ask if she knows the science behind how alcohol affects developing teenage brains and if she knows it has now been found to have a permanent effect on factors such as brain power and school performance.

Be honest about your drinking history if she asks
If you drank when young and got into sticky situations, talk about it. Say that while it's enjoyable to drink moderately as an adult, there are downsides, such as hangovers, silly behavior, sickness, and a health impact.

In the long term

Help her resist peer pressure
Acknowledge it's hard for her to say no. Equip her with scripts such as, "My mum or dad will smell it on me." Make it clear that safety always comes first and that she can always ask for help in a sticky situation.

Don't get her accustomed to alcohol
Many parents believe giving teens a drink at meals helps them drink responsibly. Research shows the opposite is true and that they feel more comfortable drinking larger amounts at a younger age.

Watch your habits
Research shows that teens copy their parents' drinking habits. Limit access to alcohol at home, avoid using it as your go-to way of unwinding, and model moderate use. Emphasize that this avoids long-term health conditions. Studies show that meaningful conversations about alcohol help young people develop more sensible attitudes.

"CAN I GET
DRIVING LESSONS?"

Learning to drive has long been a rite of passage for teens. But while your teen may insist he's ready, a closer look at adolescent brain development suggests that may not be the case—which could explain why teens are four times more likely than older drivers to be involved in crashes.

SCENARIO | Your teen asks for driving lessons for his birthday.

To your teen, driving may be the ultimate badge of independence. But a wide range of research—as well as accident statistics—shows that parents would be wiser to apply the brakes. Car accidents are the leading cause of death in teens. Other studies reveal that one in four teens will be in a car crash within 6 months of learning to drive. The parts of his brain that govern good judgment and assess risk are still developing. Scans also show that risky practices, such as speeding and overtaking, trigger a stronger reaction in the pleasure center of his brain. Teens are also more likely to check phones while driving and to drive under the influence of drugs or alcohol.

WHAT YOU MIGHT
BE THINKING

You may wonder if he's mature enough for such a big step. You may also see how badly he wants to drive and think back fondly to when you passed your test.

" "

TEENS' RISKY BEHAVIOR MEANS CAUTION IS ADVISED WHEN IT COMES TO DRIVING.

WHAT HE MIGHT BE THINKING

◉ **Your teen knows** that being among the first to drive is likely to make him more in demand socially from peers who also want more freedom from adults.

◉ **Scans show that for teens**, taking risks behind the wheel— such as running red lights—feels good, not scary, because it triggers a stronger reaction in their brains' pleasure center.

◉ **At this stage**, your teen believes he's so "special" that he's invulnerable, and that while other people have accidents, it won't happen to him.

◉ **Even though he knows** he's not supposed to use his phone while driving, research has found that fear of missing out means adolescents can't resist checking their phones, even on short trips.

▶ **SEE RELATED TOPICS** ◀
Peer pressure and "FOMO": pp.58–59
You only live once: pp.198–199

HOW YOU COULD RESPOND

In the moment

Ask him to wait, if possible
As well as being more likely to take risks, your teen won't have developed some of the motor coordination or judgment that would make him a safer driver. Studies found that 17-year-olds would have 9 percent fewer crashes in their first year of driving if they waited until they were 18, and a further 8 percent fewer if they waited until they were 19.

Be more cautious with boys
Point out that teenage boys are more likely to be in a fatal car crash, possibly because higher testosterone rates make them more prone to aggressive driving, so you think it would be safer to wait.

In the long term

Drive with your teen
If he has lessons, drive with him as much as possible, praising good decisions and factually pointing out poor ones. Studies show the more involved a parent is in a teen learning to drive, the less likely he is to crash. Get him to drive on country roads and in bad weather. Teens are more likely to crash at night, so rule out night drives until he's more experienced.

Warn against phone use
Once he's passed, insist that his phone is on silent and out of sight while driving or that he installs an app that automatically blocks calls and notifications when driving.

Highlight peer pressure
Just having one friend in the car ups his crash risk by 44 percent. Consider a no-friend rule for up to a year after he starts driving.

Talk about seat belts
Young drivers are less likely to always wear seat belts, especially when with friends. Point out that 60 percent of teens who die in car accidents weren't restrained.

"I'M **GAY**."

For teens, discovering and sometimes declaring their sexual identity is an important part of becoming an adult. But for young people who aren't straight, there can be added challenges if they feel they're not conforming to a more traditional heterosexual role.

SCENARIO | Your teenager comes out to you.

Your teen may have had an idea about his sexuality for several years, but now that he's more secure in his identity, he feels ready to tell you.

Less stigma and more openness around LGBTQ+ issues today mean that young people are coming out earlier than ever; in the last two decades, the average age has fallen from 20 years old to around 16. This can be a socially vulnerable time for your teen, so it's important to keep an eye on his mental health. Supporting your teen's feelings will help make his adolescent years as secure as possible.

WHAT YOU MIGHT BE THINKING

You may wonder if your son is going through a phase of experimentation or whether he's certain about his choice. You may worry he might be affected by discrimination or homophobia or worry how other family members might react. If you didn't suspect he wasn't straight, you may wonder how you missed the signs.

WHAT HE MIGHT BE THINKING

◉ **Your teen might be worried** about how you'll react, especially if you've ever said anything that made him think you disapprove of same-sex couples.

◉ **If he's been trying to hide** his sexuality, telling you will feel like a relief. If he hasn't told others yet, he may see coming out to you as a decisive first step in being able to declare his sexuality openly to the world.

◉ **Even if he believes** you'll be supportive, he may worry about how older, more conservative members of the family, such as grandparents, might react.

◉ **Almost all male gay students** say they have heard the word "gay" used as a put-down, sometimes as a way for other boys to assert heterosexual masculinity. For this reason, he may be more nervous about coming out to his peers than to you.

SEE RELATED TOPICS
Sex and contraception: pp.110–111
Sexuality and gender: pp.120–121

HOW YOU COULD RESPOND

In the moment

Be accepting
Thank him for telling you. He'll remember this moment for the rest of his life, so be clear you're supportive and that you love him. Don't talk too much. Listen and remember that he's still the same person. If you think he'd like it, offer a sign of physical affection.

Make this moment his
Even if you feel surprised at his news and need some time to adjust your thoughts about his future, make sure that he doesn't sense this. Ensure that this remains your teen's moment and make it clear from the outset that you support him unconditionally.

In the long term

Keep talking about healthy sex
If you're heterosexual, you may feel unqualified to talk about gay sex. But the principles of safe sex, consent, and good relationships still apply. Stress the importance of wearing condoms to prevent STIs.

Talk to family members
Once you think your teen is ready, ask him when he wants to tell others in the family. How would he like to handle sharing his news with siblings and other family members? Support him during this process and help answer any questions they may have.

Create a safe haven
Homophobic bullying is the most common kind in schools, according to research, with name-calling such as "queer," "faggot," or "gay" common. Acknowledge that bullying, both verbal and sometimes physical, is a concern for your teen. Make sure that he has a consistently supportive environment at home and feels like he has a safe place to be and to bring his friends.

Be positive about LGBTQ+ issues
He'll be assessing how you really feel about him being gay. Talk positively about LGBTQ+ role models. Ask him what he'd like you to understand about his sexuality and if there are any films or books he identifies with that would help you get his feelings.

Respect his relationships
You may have had to adjust your mindset about your teen, but understand that love is love, and look forward to your teen enjoying a fulfilling and loving relationship. Accept any future partner he may have and be excited that your child is introducing you to someone so important in his life.

CHAPTER 4

YOUR
17 – 18
YEAR-OLD

"WHY DO YOU HAVE TO SPEAK TO MY TEACHER?"

Now that your teen is in his senior year of high school, he has more freedom at school. This means he may resent any interference from you when it comes to his progress at school and may want to keep you out of the loop.

SCENARIO | Your teen is mad when you ask to see his teacher after a bad report card.

Your teen is encouraged to take more responsibility for his work now. However, he may need time to develop the organizational skills and motivation to achieve his best results, especially after he sees he won't be immediately penalized for poor work. For some, this means that grades slide. It's important to find ways to stay involved that you're both happy with. Studies show that students whose parents encourage rather than interfere are more likely to succeed.

WHAT YOU MIGHT BE THINKING

You've always been able to discuss his progress with teachers, so you may be annoyed or suspicious that he's keeping you at a distance. You may not want to interfere, but feel you have to do all you can to help with his final tests, which you believe will help decide his future.

SEE RELATED TOPICS
My teacher hates me: pp.152–153
I thought it was a free period: pp.184–185

"   "

YOUR TEEN MAY QUESTION YOUR INVOLVEMENT NOW THAT HE'S MORE IN CHARGE OF WORK.

WHAT HE MIGHT BE THINKING

◉ **How open he is** about his work may depend on his achievements to date. If he hasn't done as well as he could have or has felt criticized or pushed by you in the past, he may be more secretive.

◉ **If he's not invited** to the meeting, he's likely to be paranoid about what's being said and will want the opportunity to defend himself.

◉ **It's likely your teen** has a good idea why he got a bad report card, but now that you've asked for a meeting to get to the bottom of it, he may try to deflect attention away from his grades by saying that his teacher doesn't like him.

◉ **The more worried** you get about his academic performance, the more he'll feel entitled to blame you and his teachers for pressuring him. He's more likely to complain that you're the problem as a way to deflect responsibility from himself.

HOW YOU COULD RESPOND

In the moment

Ask what's worrying him
Talk through issues that might come up. This can help bring them into sharper focus and help your teen consider solutions.

Request that he comes, too
Can you speak to his teacher on the phone first to find out the bigger picture? Then ask if your son can attend a follow-up meeting where you all brainstorm solutions.

Consider backing off
Alternatively, see if he'd like you to delay the meeting so he can address issues by himself. Asking to see his teacher sends the message that he can't improve on his own.

Tell him you're on his side
Say he's in charge of his learning but will achieve more if he sees you and his teachers as a back-up team, with him in the driver's seat.

In the long term

Discuss short- and long-term goals
Encourage him to come up with manageable short-term goals, such as adding detail to essays. Long term, ask him where he wants to be in 5 and 10 years' time. Say that what he does now will expand his choices.

Avoid labels
Resist labeling him as lazy. Instead, make it clear that with more effort, he'll always improve. Notice when he's trying harder

and emphasize effort, which is in his control, over results.

Help with organization skills
He may feel overwhelmed or unsure of how to use study time. Until his brain's executive functions of self-control and foresight mature, he may need help with skills such as time management. Say that he shouldn't worry about asking for help, as filling in learning gaps now will avoid confusion later on.

"YOU DON'T KNOW MY FRIENDS LIKE I DO."

Teens typically spend almost as much time with peers as they do with their parents or siblings. To your teenager, her circle of friends is her other family—only she's chosen them. She'll feel that any criticism of them is a criticism of her and her choices.

SCENARIO | When you say you're worried about some friends being a bad influence, your teen says that you don't know them.

As your teen starts to edge away from you toward independence, her friends help her define herself. Her terror of being cut adrift from her friend group means she'll be fiercely loyal to them, even if she privately knows you have a reason to worry about some of their behavior. If you try to manage her social life, she's likely to be more defiant and will side with them.

WHAT YOU MIGHT BE THINKING

If she's said that some of her friends drink, smoke, or engage in risky activities, or you suspect that they do, you may worry she'll be led astray. You may feel she's more interested in them than her family.

WHAT SHE MIGHT BE THINKING

◉ **As she forms** her new identity, she wants some separation and isn't ready for you to see the more grown-up person she's trying to be with her friends.

◉ **Though she wants** some distance, she also wants you to like her friends so that she can see them when she wants and invite them over without her—or them—feeling your disapproval.

◉ **She may have confided** that "others" in her group drink and smoke to test your reaction and won't admit if she took part as well. She'll regret telling you if you say they're a bad influence.

◉ **Even if she has reservations** about her friends, she'll resent any judgment. She'll defend them to the utmost, even if she knows you might be right.

▶ SEE RELATED TOPICS ◀
Peer pressure and "FOMO": pp.58–59
You always criticize: pp.148–149

HOW YOU COULD RESPOND

In the moment

Avoid criticism
If you disapprove of friends, you'll have less influence, as she won't share what's happening in her friend group.

See it as a learning curve
Though she'll make some bad choices, which may mean spending time with friends you disapprove of, say you trust her to make good decisions so she's motivated to live up to your positive expectations.

Don't assume she's an angel
She is likely to have edited out her part in any risky things she's told you her friends have done. Bear in mind that their parents may have heard similar things about your teen.

Offer yourself as an excuse
If you fear her friends put her in risky situations, give her a code word so she can call you anytime she's in an uncomfortable position and wants you to pick her up.

In the long term

Open up your home
By offering your teen's friends a place to meet, you'll get to understand her friendships better. The more welcome her friends feel, the more influence you'll have.

Help her resist peer pressure
You're likely to feel better about her hanging out with her friends if she has the skills to stand up for herself. Talk through scenarios where she might be tested to do something against her better judgment. Equip her with simple but assertive phrases such as, "This isn't my kind of thing," so she can make her boundaries clear.

Remain her biggest influence
Invest the time to stay close to her so your family remains the main group she wants to belong to. Also, research shows that once teens leave home, their decisions about sex and drinking are linked more to their family's values than their friends'. Share and explain yours.

"I THOUGHT IT WAS A FREE PERIOD."

As your teen gets to the end of high school, she'll find her timetable is less tightly scheduled. Sometimes teens may take advantage of this freedom to skip classes. If this happens regularly, it's important to work with her to understand her reasons.

SCENARIO | Your teen says she thought she had a free period when the school says she missed a class.

There could be many reasons why your teen missed a class. She may enjoy the thrill of breaking rules or want to fit in with peers doing so. Timetable changes may mean she's made a mistake or feels too embarrassed to ask for help. If she struggles academically, she may be disillusioned with school.

It's possible she may also feel disliked by a teacher, has not done her homework, or is being teased by classmates. Or, if she's confident about her ability, she may feel she's old enough to decide how she learns best. In all cases, help her see the effect missing classes now could have on her future.

WHAT YOU MIGHT BE THINKING

You're likely to be more frustrated if she's skipped classes often. Whatever the reason, you may feel unable to trust her, worried about the effect on her studies, and concerned you'll be held responsible by the school.

◥ **SEE RELATED TOPICS** ◣
I'm telling the truth: pp.144–145
My teacher hates me: pp.152–153

" "
WITH A MORE FLEXIBLE TIMETABLE, YOUR TEEN MAY FEEL SHE CAN TAKE CONTROL.

WHAT SHE MIGHT BE THINKING

⊚ **If she didn't do well** on tests, she may feel that it's too late to improve and that school is a waste of time. If she's struggling or feels negatively labeled by a teacher, she may be avoiding classes.

⊚ **Her brain development** means she still doesn't see the consequences of missing classes clearly. If she was skipping a class with friends, she knows she'll probably be found out but enjoys the short-term reward she gets from her risky behavior and fitting in with like-minded peers.

⊚ **If she's self-directed** and does well academically, she may want to take more charge of her learning. If she doesn't respect a teacher, she may believe their classes aren't useful. Or, if she has only a couple classes that day, she may think it's pointless to go in.

⊚ **If friends** have different free periods, she may worry they're hanging out without her and she's missing out.

HOW YOU COULD RESPOND

In the moment

Get perspective and stay calm
Schools' target attendance records mean that many send automatic messages if they think a pupil has been absent without permission. Although you may be upset with her, don't jump to conclusions. Approach the subject when you're calm. Was there confusion over her timetable, or did she think a teacher was absent? If you find she missed her class deliberately, be clear you want to understand her reasons to help her address them.

Intervene quickly
If you discover she misses classes regularly, get involved immediately so you can help break the cycle. The more she misses, the harder it will be for her to catch up and the less she'll want to attend classes.

In the long term

Work with the school
If she struggles with a teacher or you suspect she has undiagnosed social, emotional, or learning issues, it's crucial to work with the school to help her. Let them know you'll keep a watchful eye on her.

Encourage her
If she has lost confidence because of poor results, give her a "growth mindset." Say that every class improves her mastery of a subject. Suggest she competes with herself, not with classmates.

Discuss peer pressure
Acknowledge that it will take willpower to stand up to friends skipping classes. Role-play scripts to help her say "no."

Show your belief in education
If you've taken her out of classes for flimsy reasons in the past or allowed skip days when she didn't feel like going in, she may think that school can be optional. Reversing this belief takes time. Emphasize your belief in the importance of regular attendance.

"CAN I GET MY **LIPS DONE?**"

Teens want to look good to feel good and constantly compare looks. Image-based social media now makes it even easier for your teen to make comparisons. She may notice that others use more radical means than just makeup to improve their looks and wonder if she needs to do the same.

SCENARIO | Your teen says she wants lip fillers after a friend's older sister gets her lips done.

Your daughter is likely to see carefully crafted selfies of both friends and celebrities constantly on social media. One of the most easily compared features is the size and shape of lips. She may know of celebrities who got lip fillers at a young age and went on to enjoy a worldwide social media following. Combined with this, lip filler treatments are now offered more readily for increasingly affordable prices, so she may feel that such a transformation is within reach.

WHAT YOU MIGHT BE THINKING

You may feel sad that she already feels "not good enough" and worry that fillers could go wrong. You may feel torn if she insists she needs bigger lips to make her feel confident.

WHAT SHE MIGHT BE THINKING

⊚ **Research shows** that when teens—especially girls—look at social media, they experience "the contrast effect." Seeing lots of images of peers she believes are more attractive makes her more self-critical. Also, studies have found that even when teens know images have been enhanced, they still compare themselves to them. She may be aspiring to look like something that isn't real.

⊚ **To convince you**, she may say that "everyone" does it, even if she knows only one or two teens who've enlarged their lips. She may also say it's risk-free and no more serious than having highlights.

⊚ **If she hears** self-critical voices, she may believe lip fillers are what she needs to feel confident and is blocking out warnings about risks.

◀ **SEE RELATED TOPICS** ▶
Peer pressure and "FOMO": pp.58–59
All my friends look amazing: pp.122–123

" "

SOCIAL MEDIA COMPARISONS CAN MAKE COSMETIC ENHANCEMENTS DESIRABLE.

HOW YOU COULD RESPOND

In the moment

Listen
You might be tempted to say "no" immediately, but this will make her feel misunderstood and not listened to. Thank her for telling you. Ask how she feels about her looks and why she thinks lip fillers might make her more attractive.

Talk through the consequences
Without lecturing, help her consider other issues. How will she afford it? What happens if it goes wrong or her lips look strange? Explain that lip fillers were originally designed to restore volume lost with age and can look odd on young people. Help her see that her lips are in proportion to her face now.

Mention noninvasive alternatives
Suggest safe ways to experiment. Could she try lip-lining techniques, different lipstick shades, or plumping lip glosses that stimulate blood circulation?

In the long term

Remind her that she isn't a product
Constantly assessing how she looks on social media and comparing herself with others can make your daughter feel like a product. This in turn makes her more likely to be depressed, and it has been found that when girls judge their worth on how they look, it has other side effects, such as performing poorly on tests. Help her be kinder to herself and notice what she likes about the way she looks.

Explore ethics
Discuss how cosmetic fillers are tested on animals to help her understand the impact of her decision.

Talk through the bigger picture
Point out how, throughout history, social pressures have tried to make women conform to certain looks. Mention equality, too. Do boys go through the same discomfort to look good?

ANXIETY AND DEPRESSION

Every teen worries and feels down from time to time. However, if these feelings start to interfere seriously with a teenager's daily life, they may be developing symptoms of anxiety or depression.

Teens can develop anxiety when they overestimate a threat, such as how poorly they'll do on a test, and don't believe they can cope. Depression is a low mood that lasts for weeks, accompanied by symptoms such as feelings of helplessness and worthlessness, changes in appetite and energy, excessive crying, and having trouble sleeping. If your teen is anxious or depressed, listen without criticism. Let them express painful emotions and talk about times in the past when they've overcome problems. Remind them that feelings pass and life can always improve.

1

Discuss stress and anxiety
Explain how these differ. Your teen may not know the difference between stress, which is a normal response to everyday challenges, and anxiety, which interferes with normal functioning.

4

Challenge negative voices
Teens are prone to self-critical thinking, which can drive depression and anxiety. Help your teen challenge these voices and replace them with the counsel of a kind or wise friend.

6

Keep teens involved
If your teen is withdrawing, this feeds anxiety and depression. Plan something for them to do each day out of the house, such as walking the dog or running an errand.

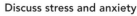

WORKING THINGS OUT

8 key principles

2

Talk about effects on the brain
Explain that anxiety is triggered when the brain overestimates a threat. It goes into high alert and sends messages to increase stress hormones in the body. Your teen may feel no longer in control, but deep breathing and calm thoughts can help manage their response.

3

Teach teens to check stress levels
Suggest they imagine a sliding scale from 1 to 10. When your teen feels close to an 8, they could take steps to de-stress, such as getting outside for some exercise, which has proven benefits.

5

Avoid screen isolation
Research shows that 48 percent of teens who spend 5 or more hours a day on devices have higher rates of depression, possibly because they're dealing with worries alone. Can your teen avoid constant news feeds and online comparisons? Frame screen-free time as a reward.

7

Manage stress levels
Stress trickles down from parents to children—animal and human studies show that when parents are stressed, their offspring are stressed, too. Make your home a haven and create regular family time to send the message that the world is a safe place.

8

Explain perfection isn't possible
Say you're not perfect and don't expect them to be either. By giving them permission to scrap unrealistic targets, they can stop feeling that they're falling short and be kinder to themselves.

!

TAILORED ADVICE

Age by age

13–14
YEAR-OLDS

Build emotional vocabulary
Set a challenge to learn a new "feeling" word each week. Help your teen rate emotions from 1 to 10 to assess their intensity.

Avoid isolation
Now that teens can join social networks, keep them involved in family life rather than leave them to look at screens alone.

15–16
YEAR-OLDS

Monitor sleep
Don't be lax on bedtimes. Not getting enough sleep over time increases the risk of anxiety and depression.

Check your anxieties
Don't pass on your concerns that anxiety and depression could affect their tests.

17–18
YEAR-OLDS

Talk about success
If test results were disappointing, say there are many ways to succeed. Practical skills or activities, such as volunteering, can make teens feel competent.

Help with heartache
A relationship break-up can trigger depression. Encourage your teen to allow for grieving time to process sad feelings.

"I'M TAKING A YEAR OFF."

By this age, your teenager is likely to have been in nonstop education most of her life. She may have felt under considerable pressure to get good grades at the end of high school, but she may also feel she'd like time out before the next chapter of her education.

SCENARIO | Your teen says that she's thinking of taking a year off before college.

A year off is a step into the unknown and a departure from the linear academic track she's been on, so your teen may be nervous about mentioning the idea. However, a body of research shows that a year off can help your teen clarify her passions and goals and cope better at college. Colleges also find that students who've taken a year off are more likely to start their courses focused, engaged, and motivated. As college anxiety levels climb, many also endorse a break as a way to build resilience. But a break can also slow her academic and career momentum, so she'll need to think carefully about her priorities.

WHAT YOU MIGHT BE THINKING

You may worry that she's wasting time and wonder how she'll fund it. In a competitive world, you may feel she should get on with the next stage of her life. You may also worry about her safety if traveling.

◆ **SEE RELATED TOPICS** ◆
I miss you: pp.206–207
Sorry you haven't heard from me: pp.212–213

WHAT SHE MIGHT BE THINKING

⊚ **Your teen may feel** that she's been told what to do by adults all of her life and that now it's time to make her own decisions, free from expectations. After so much focus on tests, she may also feel she needs a break to rediscover her love of learning.

⊚ **She may think that** she has yet to stretch herself and take herself out of her comfort zone. She may also want to earn her own money so she won't be under as much financial pressure at college.

⊚ **A year off** could be her way of sorting out conflicting feelings about going into further education and what degree she wants to do. She may want to dip her toe into the world of work or try an apprenticeship to see whether she'd rather start her career earlier.

" "

A PLANNED YEAR OFF CAN BE AN OPPORTUNITY FOR TEENS TO RECHARGE AND REFOCUS.

HOW YOU COULD RESPOND

In the moment

Listen to her reasons
This is an important moment for her to assert her independence. Show you have faith in her ability to plan.

Avoid thinking of a year off as a diversion
Not all education happens in classrooms. During a well-planned, challenging year off, your teen is likely to improve skills such as leadership and problem-solving.

Give your side
Be clear that at such a formative time of life, she needs to make the most of her time. While it's her choice, say you'd expect her to structure a year off around activities based on her interests but that also build life skills.

Suggest she secures her college place first
A year off is likely to be more stress-free if she is accepted at a college first and then asks to defer entry rather than tries to apply when she's no longer at school.

In the long term

Don't rush the transition
Consider whether she has the skills yet to thrive at college. Look out for clues that she needs time to mature, such as disorganization or not looking after herself. Accept it if she's unsure altogether about college. Ask if she's reconsidering it and listen to her reasons. There are many ways to be successful in life.

Put risks into perspective
You may be worried if she's planning to travel. But while travel accidents make the news, in reality, teens aren't significantly more at risk abroad than at home. If you think she needs it, suggest a short travel safety course.

Check her well-being
Most teens have some idea of what they want to do on a year off. If she seems chronically unmotivated, consider whether she's experiencing depression or any dependency problems she may need help with.

"CAN **YOU DO IT?**"

Although your teen wants independence, he isn't always sure about going it alone, especially when he knows you'll do difficult tasks for him. However, stepping in constantly can affect his confidence in the long term.

SCENARIO | Your teen asks you to fill in his college application form.

It's natural to want to protect your teenager from stress and disappointment. Today's parents tend to want to help out more because we worry more about teens' stress levels and mental health. We also believe that because there's more competition for higher education and jobs, we should lend a helping hand. However, childhood is a process of learning, and if you do too much for your teen, he may doubt his own ability to work things out.

WHAT YOU MIGHT BE THINKING

You may think it's easier if you fill in the forms "correctly." You may also want to relieve his workload. You may worry that other teens' parents are helping with applications, so yours will lose out if you don't help.

HOW YOU COULD RESPOND

In the moment

Give him training
Talk him through how to fill in the form. Ask him to read the questions carefully, check what references are required, and consider how long he'll need. Explain that while you're happy to look over the completed form, this is a helpful training exercise.

He can expect it to be challenging at times, but that's part of the process.

Expect opposition
If you're often his personal assistant, he won't want to give that up. Say you have faith in him now to do more.

In the long term

Keep the end goal in mind
Our ultimate goal as parents is to create children who can stand on their own two feet, especially as the cost of mistakes gets more serious as he gets older—for example, if he misses a work deadline. Even if you find it hard to watch, he has to be able to get frustrated and push on through to learn lessons and feel competent.

Brainstorm solutions
Instead of constantly directing, ask what he thinks he should do. More often than not, he'll come up with a practical, age-appropriate answer.

Study your thoughts
When a challenging situation arises, think, "Could he do this himself?" If the answer is yes, let him do it. If it's no, give him some skills so that next time he can go it alone.

Praise his competence
The ability to take on and master challenges is one of the main building blocks of self-esteem. Acknowledge each achievement.

Build his skills
Find ways for him to do more form-filling and organizing, such as making appointments. He'll enjoy the sense of achievement.

WHAT HE MIGHT BE THINKING

◉ **If you've always** stepped in to do tricky tasks, he's probably happy to let you continue doing so.

◉ **He knows** he's almost old enough to leave home, but he may not yet feel like an adult or believe you think he's mature. Research shows that only 16 percent of 18–25-year-olds say they feel they've reached adulthood.

◉ **He could be happy to use** your concern that he might get stressed to let you continue doing the tasks he finds daunting or inconvenient.

◉ **When you do a hard task** for him, it can make him feel that he can't do anything as well as you can and that you don't believe he's capable.

SEE RELATED TOPICS
I've got too much to do: pp.52–53
Help! I'm already late!: pp.158–159

CONSTANTLY STEPPING IN CAN MAKE TEENS FEEL LESS CAPABLE.

"CAN MY BOYFRIEND SLEEP OVER?"

By this age, teens are moving toward more serious relationships. However, if your child asks you if their partner can stay the night, it can feel like a dilemma if you're still getting used to the idea of her being sexually active.

SCENARIO | Your teen asks if her partner can stay over.

Some parents may struggle with the idea of their teenager being sexually active because it requires a big shift in the view we have of our children as innocent. It doesn't seem long ago that they were little, so we instinctively worry they're not ready to take part in this adult activity. Parents, particularly fathers, tend to find it harder to accept a daughter's burgeoning sexuality than a son's, even though by this age girls are increasingly sexually confident. How you react may also depend on your sexual history as a teenager, what your parents allowed, and your personal values.

WHAT YOU MIGHT BE THINKING

You may feel instinctively uncomfortable with them sleeping under the same roof but find it hard to express this. If you say yes, you may worry you're giving tacit permission for her to have sex.

SEE RELATED TOPICS

Sex and contraception: pp.110–111
We're going out together: pp.170–171

WHAT SHE MIGHT BE THINKING

• **If they're already** having sex, her request may signal that she's tired of lying and hiding evidence such as condom wrappers. She wants to feel comfortable having her boyfriend over.

• **She may resent** your assumption that they're unable to control themselves for one night. She may also feel awkward with the idea of having sex with you nearby.

• **She may want recognition** that she's in a legit relationship. If you object, she may say you're old-fashioned or treating her like a child. She may also think that you disapprove of her boyfriend.

• **Depending on your relationship** and her personality, if you insist he sleeps in a separate room, she may find it challenging and exciting to find a way to have sex anyway.

" "

ADJUSTING TO YOUR TEEN BEING SEXUALLY ACTIVE CAN BE DIFFICULT.

HOW YOU COULD RESPOND

In the moment

Talk about it
Thank her for asking you. Rather than say no immediately, ask her to talk through the reasons. You may feel protective, but if you have no moral objection, try to see it as part of her learning curve as she moves toward adulthood.

Ask for more time if you need it
It can take time to accept that she's a sexual being. Tell her you need to adjust to the idea and get to know him better before he shares your home.

Discuss protection and mutual enjoyment
As well as discussing the risks of getting pregnant or STIs, talk about the importance of mutual investment, trust, and care. Research shows that teens who have a positive, open discussion about sex with parents use contraception better, have fewer partners, and are less likely to get pregnant.

In the long term

Examine your beliefs
Do you think that boys only want sex and that girls are more likely to be hurt? Teens have been found to behave more responsibly and learn better relationship skills when parents accept they're having sex as part of a loving relationship.

Decide on any boundaries
Consider boundaries, such as asking that her boyfriend respects house rules and leaving her bedroom door open during the day.

Make it clear sex is private
Explain that sex is an intimate act between two people and that if they're sleeping together under your roof, you'd like them to be considerate and discreet.

CONSENT

Teens may know a lot about the mechanics of sex, but as they start to have relationships, they still need guidance on mutual respect and issues such as sexual abuse and harassment.

Research shows that parents are the most powerful sex educators children have. Even though conversations may feel awkward at first, the messages parents give are key in helping teenagers understand the importance of boundaries. They're on a steep learning curve, so you should discuss issues before your teen starts to explore sexually with a partner, and return to the topic again and again. The bottom line is to tell your teen to do things only that they and their partner both feel comfortable and enthusiastic about.

" "
THE MESSAGES PARENTS GIVE THEIR TEENS ARE KEY TO THEIR UNDERSTANDING OF BOUNDARIES.

1
Help teens practice consent
Give them control over their bodies from an early age, asking if they want to be hugged and kissed. Help them stand up for themselves in other contexts, too—for example, when a friend puts pressure on them.

4
Be gender-balanced
Parents tend to describe a victim–predator dynamic between girls and boys. But boys can also feel sexual pressure from both genders. Boys and girls should expect to give, and get, consent.

6
Talk about intimacy
Discuss how sex is more enjoyable if there's an emotional connection and both partners respect and trust one another.

WORKING THINGS OUT

8 key principles

2

Get teens to trust their instincts
Teens can feel they have to be accommodating to be liked. Encourage self-examination—for example, "Do I feel comfortable with this?"

3

Talk about balance
If a partner always wants to know where they are and is angry if they don't like the answers, do they feel like it's a balanced relationship?

5

Discuss alcohol and drugs
Say that drinking alcohol and taking drugs makes it hard to defend yourself, disinhibits, and how consent cannot be given if intoxicated.

7

Share experiences
If it feels appropriate, be prepared to talk about your own first experiences. Talk about the benefits of waiting until both parties can be open and honest enough to say what they want.

8

Reframe consent
Consent is key, but explain that sex is more than just gaining permission; it's about mutual enjoyment. Talk about it as "enthusiastic agreement" for both parties. Suggest ways to ask open-ended questions such as, "Do you want to …?" Explain that they can say "no" to stop an activity at any point.

"YOU ONLY **LIVE ONCE.**"

During adolescence, young people take more risks than at any other time of life. Teenage brains are wired to get more of a kick from risk-taking for many reasons, not least that it triggers the release of more of the feel-good chemical messenger dopamine than it does in adults.

SCENARIO | You overhear your teen's friends reliving a dangerous challenge he did. When you ask him why he did it, he replies, "You only live once."

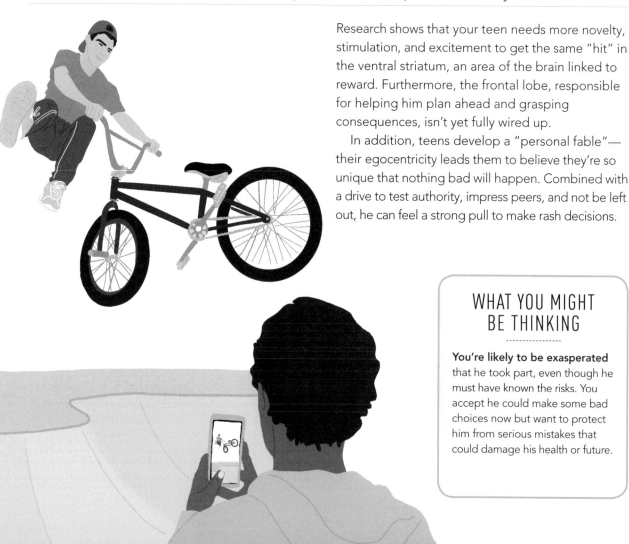

Research shows that your teen needs more novelty, stimulation, and excitement to get the same "hit" in the ventral striatum, an area of the brain linked to reward. Furthermore, the frontal lobe, responsible for helping him plan ahead and grasping consequences, isn't yet fully wired up.

In addition, teens develop a "personal fable"—their egocentricity leads them to believe they're so unique that nothing bad will happen. Combined with a drive to test authority, impress peers, and not be left out, he can feel a strong pull to make rash decisions.

WHAT YOU MIGHT BE THINKING

You're likely to be exasperated that he took part, even though he must have known the risks. You accept he could make some bad choices now but want to protect him from serious mistakes that could damage his health or future.

" "

A LACK OF PLANNING AHEAD AND A DESIRE FOR A QUICK "HIT" WIRES TEENS FOR RISK-TAKING.

WHAT HE MIGHT BE THINKING

⊙ **While your teen** probably knows he shouldn't have accepted the challenge, the fact that he was with friends made him do it. Studies show that teens are more likely to indulge in risky behavior when peers are present.

⊙ **Even though he's likely** to have clearly understood the risks, research shows how, in the moment, the reward of the thrill and impressing friends can be enough to outweigh any misgivings.

⊙ **The sensitivity of his brain** to the neurotransmitter dopamine, which is released in the run-up to taking a risk, means the act gave him powerful feelings of being alive and invincible.

HOW YOU COULD RESPOND

In the moment

See it in context
While nerve-wracking for you, risk-taking is believed to serve an evolutionary purpose, allowing teens to explore the outside world, still under your protection.

Help him learn from his mistakes
Rather than shame him, talk through what happened and what led him to the decision so that he can make better choices in future.

In the long term

Discuss peer pressure
He's likely to make better choices if he recognizes peer pressure. Prepare him for dilemmas with phrases such as, "I don't feel like it"or "No, I'm not into it." Or he could use you as an excuse, saying, "My parents would ground me."

Talk about pausing
Suggest he takes time out to assess a risky situation. Removing himself, whether to send a text or to go to the bathroom, gives him time to check his gut feelings.

Discuss "hot" and "cold" contexts
"Hot" contexts are decisions made in the heat of the moment, fueled

by peer pressure, excitement, or a need for validation. "Cold" contexts are more logical decisions taken in the cold light of day. Helping him recognize the difference will remind him to step back and use more of his rational thinking. Talk about how there's plenty of ways to enjoy adrenaline- and dopamine-boosting activities while staying safe.

Discuss alcohol and drugs
After as little as 1 ounce, alcohol decreases activity in the part of his brain that helps him think rationally and realize he's gone too far. His risk of injury also multiplies sixfold when he uses alcohol or drugs.

◀ **SEE RELATED TOPICS** ▶
Peer pressure and "FOMO": pp.58–59
Drugs: pp.202–203

"I'M GETTING **A TATTOO**."

Tattoos are undeniably more mainstream nowadays, but the permanence, possible health risks, and worries about how others view them means your teen's announcement that she's getting a tattoo could be a difficult moment.

SCENARIO | Your teen shows you a tattoo design she plans to have done.

Like piercings, tattoos draw a visible line between childhood and adulthood because of the way they proclaim, "I choose what to do with my body and how I express myself." There are also developmental reasons tattoos appeal to teens. Adolescents release more of the reward chemical dopamine when they do something daring. Also, the brain's frontal lobe, which helps us foresee the consequences of actions, isn't fully wired up until the mid-twenties. In any case, the devil-may-care connotations associated with body art are likely to be a big part of the attraction.

WHAT YOU MIGHT BE THINKING

You may feel she'll "defile" her body and be upset she wants to brand herself permanently. How you feel may also be affected by the tattoo's design, size, and intended location. If you've previously disapproved of tattoos, you may feel she's rejecting your values.

❝ ❞

FOR TEENS, GETTING A TATTOO IS A WAY TO BE IN CONTROL OF THEIR BODY.

WHAT SHE MIGHT BE THINKING

⊙ **She feels invulnerable** and wants to be seen as daring by peers. She wants her tattoo to symbolize her youthful passion and to immortalize beliefs or interests that mean a lot to her now.

⊙ **She's just experienced** many physical changes. Getting a tattoo is one alteration she believes she can control. If she's unhappy with a part of her body, having a tattoo there may distract her from those painful feelings and give her a reason to display that area again.

⊙ **If you strongly disapprove**, she'll believe that you're out of touch or don't understand her reasons. She may think that you should let go.

⊙ **As a tattoo** feels rebellious in the first place, if you try to forbid one or react emotionally, this may reinforce her desire to get one.

HOW YOU COULD RESPOND

In the moment

Be clear on the law
If she's under 18, make it clear it's illegal for her to have a tattoo and that she'll have to wait to get one.

Suspend judgment
Don't instantly assume that she doesn't know what she's doing. Accusing her of making an irrational decision is likely to make her more determined. Thank her for telling you and aim instead to have several chats to explore the pros and cons.

Show genuine interest
Ask about the design, why it feels important, and if she's researched its meaning if it's a symbol or saying. Is there a middle ground, such as a small back tattoo, that satisfies her desire for a tattoo but lets her choose when to display it?

Suggest a compromise
Could she agree to wait a while and save money to pay for it? This allows her to be sure and shows you she's serious.

In the long term

Acknowledge changing times
Tattoos no longer carry the stigma they once did. Accepting times have changed will make her more likely to listen to your point of view.

Talk about future choices
If she wants to get rid of a tattoo later on, laser removal is pricey and difficult. Say how we evolve in life and interests change. Ask her to think about how quickly she's changing and evolving.

Explore the health risks
Check all the risks together, from bleeding to allergic reactions to hepatitis and HIV, so she can't say you're exaggerating. If she wants to proceed, she needs to find a well-respected, professional parlor with the highest hygiene standards.

Watch for a progression
If she continues to get large, visible tattoos that you think could be a form of self-harm, you may need to explore her reasons more, possibly with professional help. Also, for some teens, the buzz of getting a tattoo can be addictive. If she seems unable to stop, give her the support she needs.

◀ **SEE RELATED TOPICS** ▶
Self-harm: pp.78–79
All my friends dye their hair: pp.112–113

DRUGS

As parents, our instinct is to tell teens that all drugs
are dangerous and that they should "just say no."
However, with a greater variety of drugs available
than in the past, you may worry about where to start.

Even if you're confused, it's important
to talk to teens about drugs because
statistics show that many adolescents
will come into contact with them.
Despite warnings, some teens still try
them because they're at a stage of life

when they're curious about the hype,
enjoy risk-taking, and want to fit in. It's
vital to remember that, as a parent, you
remain the key influence over whether
your teen occasionally experiments or
uses drugs more regularly.

1

Chat little and often
Rather than have one big talk,
chat as questions come up.
Be clear you don't condone
drug use, but also listen to
your teen's viewpoint.

4

Discuss the teenage brain
Let your teen know that
their age and the fact that
their brain is still developing
but learns quickly means
they can get addicted
faster than an adult.

6

Teach the skills to say "no"
Talk about peer pressure.
Role play situations to give
your teen practice saying no.
Say they can always use
you as an excuse, claiming
their strict parents will
drug test them!

WORKING THINGS OUT

8 key principles

2
Don't exaggerate
If you say that all drugs are addictive and can kill, your teen will tune out, concluding you're ignorant because they'll know peers who are well and not hooked.

3
Feel qualified
With so many new drugs around, you may worry you'll lose authority if your teen knows more than you do. Research the topic if necessary. Remember that you are the expert on your child.

5
Give perspective
While your teen may believe that "everyone" is trying drugs, figures show this isn't the case, and that drug-taking is talked about more in teen circles than actually done.

7
Answer questions
Many parents worry about being put on the spot if their teen asks if they've tried drugs and they have. See their queries not as an attempt to catch you out, but as their way of trying to understand conflicting information. Avoid too much detail or being nostalgic. Instead, emphasize why you make different decisions now.

8
Discuss marijuana
Apart from alcohol, pot is the number-one drug teens try. Even if it's legal in some places, say how, like cigarettes, that doesn't mean it's not harmful. Talk through some of the possible consequences, such as mood swings, poorer academic achievement, and altered decision-making. Point out that the risks outweigh the benefits.

TAILORED ADVICE

Age by age

13–14
YEAR-OLDS

Start talking
Teens are more impulsive now and less supervised. Start discussing drugs, even if you think your teen is too young to access them.

Be in sync with school
A message is more effective if it's repeated at school and home. Reinforce the school's teaching.

15–16
YEAR-OLDS

Check your pills
Test stress may lead some teens to see if pills in the medicine cabinet relax them. Monitor medications.

Be welcoming
Your teen is more likely to take drugs when out with friends. Get to know their friends and welcome them.

17–18
YEAR-OLDS

Choose your moment
Teens have more access to drugs now. If you see signs of use, such as slurred speech, red eyes, clenched teeth, or hyperactivity, chat calmly when they've come down from any effects.

See it in context
Teens who take drugs are likely to be experimenting and to stop by themselves. If it seems they can't, get help.

"WE **BROKE UP**."

Although teenagers' feelings can be intense, the likelihood is that your teen's first love won't last. Devastating as this can feel, his first break-up can be an important way for him to learn how to heal from difficult experiences and manage emotional pain.

SCENARIO | When you ask why you haven't seen your teen's girlfriend after noticing he's been looking sad, he tells you she broke it off.

Whether a first relationship felt like true love or was a brief summer romance, its ending will be upsetting for a teen who has never dealt with a break-up. Most teen break-ups occur because of differing needs, directions, and expectations of intimacy, or cheating.

At this stage, his self-worth is more reliant on what others think of him, and if he was rejected, this feels particularly hurtful. He may feel overwhelmed because his brain is more sensitive to hormonal and chemical changes now. He's also hypersensitive to social exclusion—a break-up signals lack of approval by a peer, so it's likely to cause intense feelings of sadness and anxiety. All of this may be why studies have found that break-ups are a leading cause of psychological distress in young people.

WHAT YOU MIGHT BE THINKING

Your reaction will depend on how long your teen's relationship was, how well you got to know his girlfriend, and how good you thought she was for him. As you know that only a few early relationships last, you may feel that he also needs to be realistic and not mope around.

◀ **SEE RELATED TOPICS** ▶
We're going out together: pp.170–171
Can my boyfriend sleep over?: pp.194–195

" "

THOUGH DEVASTATING, RELATIONSHIP BREAK-UPS HELP TEENS LEARN HOW TO MANAGE EMOTIONAL PAIN.

WHAT HE MIGHT BE THINKING

◉ **His relationship** was an important part of his development and a key step toward independence. If it's the first time he shared intimate thoughts and experiences, his rejection may feel especially hard.

◉ **Brain scans show** that withdrawal of romantic love triggers the same brain activity as withdrawal from opioids, so his pain may feel physical.

◉ **Even though** the relationship may seem brief to you, it may have been one of the defining experiences in his life so far. Because he has little long-term perspective, he may wonder if there's something wrong with him and if he'll ever find love again.

◉ **After a break-up**, many teens block their ex or delete or untag them from pictures. Losing that constant connection can make a break-up feel even more significant and lonely.

HOW YOU COULD RESPOND

In the moment

Take his feelings seriously
You may feel confident he'll move on, but he feels bereft. In a study of teen break-ups, 52 percent had symptoms of depression, which can include difficulty sleeping and intrusive thoughts. Say how, though it feels painful now, he'll eventually be able to put his loss in the past.

Look at the pros and cons
To deter him from idealizing the relationship, suggest he list its pros and cons and focuses on the positives of breaking up—such as seeing friends more and avoiding painful fights. Writing feelings down can help him gain perspective and heal sooner.

Warn against monitoring his ex
Advise him against checking up on his ex on social media, which will prolong his heartbreak. A clean break will help him resist contacting her in a weak moment and move on more quickly.

In the long term

Say it may take time
Discuss the five stages of grief: denial, anger, bargaining, depression, and acceptance. This helps him learn he'll go through a process that's essential for healing. Tell him to watch for when he feels anger so he's not tempted to retaliate by posting pictures or sending messages.

Remove mementos
Suggest he consolidates his memories, archives photos, and reorganizes his room to put reminders of the relationship out of sight so he doesn't dwell on his ex. Most pictures reflect happier times, so they could make him idealize his relationship.

Help him look after himself
Rather than listen to self-critical voices telling him what he did wrong, suggest he thinks about what advice a good friend might give. Encourage him, too, to sleep, eat well, and exercise, as it's easier to feel better emotionally and manage psychological pain if he's physically strong.

"I MISS YOU."

Moving away from home can be a big transition for a young person. Your teen may have more independence and freedom now, and it may come as a surprise to both of you if he finds it hard to settle into college life and feels homesick.

SCENARIO | A few weeks into college, your teen texts to say he misses you.

For most teenagers, college is the first time in their life they have lived away from home. So when your child says he's missing you, he's also missing the familiar routines and security he has grown up with for the last 18 years.

The stressful race to win friends and show that he fits in means that, more than ever, he yearns for predictable things that make him feel safe. Technology can also hamper his adjustment. If he's able to contact you at any time, it may take longer to make the necessary separation from home and immerse himself in college life. Social media and video games also make it easier for him to stay in his room rather than go out and meet new people.

WHAT YOU MIGHT BE THINKING

You'll know it probably took a lot for him to say this. With a rise in student depression and anxiety, you may worry about his wellness or fear he'll drop out. You may think you didn't prepare him and feel unable to help if he's far away.

SEE RELATED TOPICS
Can you do it?: pp.192–193
Sorry you haven't heard from me: pp.212–213

WHAT HE MIGHT BE THINKING

◉ **Now that he's left home**, your teen needs to find his new group, but at the moment, none of his friends feels like "family." Without familiar routines or support, he can feel very alone at times.

◉ **Having heard that college** is "the best time of your life," he could have high expectations. He may think that every day should be a wild party, and social media may lead him to believe everyone else is having more fun than him.

◉ **A bout of homesickness** may be triggered by a particular event. He may have gotten a bad grade or felt momentarily lonely or excluded.

◉ **If he's always struggled** with separation or has never spent much time away from home, he's likely to find it harder to transition.

HOW YOU COULD RESPOND

In the moment

Thank him for telling you
The teenage years are a process of separation, so it will have taken a lot for him to tell you he's struggling to settle in. Listen to his reasons and acknowledge it's been an admission for him.

Remind him it's a process
He isn't comfortable yet with his new life. Talk about how starting at college is like getting into a cold swimming pool. At first it feels freezing, but as he gets used to it, the temperature starts to feel more comfortable. Each day, get him to notice how he's spending less time thinking about home.

Talk about other times he coped
Remind him of how he made friends at school. Say he hasn't lost a home, but gained a second one.

Remind him it's normal
Research shows that up to 30 percent of students feel homesick in their first year. Knowing this can help him. Can he also talk to other students who know how it feels?

In the long term

Suggest home comforts
Having familiar things around him (while keeping his room at home intact) can help him feel more at ease. Getting to know the town or campus where he's based will also make him feel less lost.

Encourage problem-solving
If he calls constantly for practical help, get him to think through the answers. Always fixing his problems implies he can't go it alone.

Encourage small steps
Say that everyone else is seeking friends. Small gestures, such as asking someone to go for coffee, staying busy, and joining groups will help him meet others he likes.

Don't always ask what's wrong
This sends the message that you expect him to find it hard to cope. Be a good listener, but differentiate between venting—which is like releasing a pressure valve— and genuine upset.

> **BEING AWAY FROM YOU AND ALL HIS FAMILIAR ROUTINES CAN MAKE YOUR TEEN'S TRANSITION INTO COLLEGE LIFE TOUGH.**

"VAPING ISN'T BAD FOR YOU."

While the number of teens who smoke is falling, many are trying a new alternative—electronic cigarettes. Many young people believe this is healthier than smoking, but teenagers may need to find out more about the risks so they can fully understand the impact of vaping.

SCENARIO | You spot your teen vaping. Confronted at home, she says it's safe.

To your teen, vaping offers the novelty of smoking without several downsides. She can still rebel against adult authority because it's illegal to sell e-cigarettes and vaporizing liquids to anyone under 18. At the same time, it's harder to detect because it doesn't smell of tobacco. It's claimed vaping is safer than cigarettes, but a growing number of studies are highlighting risks. Many liquids contain nicotine (as well as other toxins), which can slow brain development and affect focus, self-control, learning, and mood. Some studies show vaping may be more addictive than cigarettes, can cause lung disease, and are a gateway to cigarette use.

WHAT YOU MIGHT BE THINKING

Part of you may be relieved she isn't smoking cigarettes. However, you may be confused about the health effects of vaping or about what's in the solutions—and how much nicotine they contain.

SEE RELATED TOPICS

I don't know how those cigarettes got into my bag: pp.156–157

WHAT SHE MIGHT BE THINKING

⊚ **Vaping may be exciting** to your teen if it gives her the thrill of defying authority. Compact vaporizers look like flash drives, so she can easily hide them and take a quick hit at home, at school, and even during classes.

⊚ **Surveys show** that teens think they're vaping harmless "flavors," but in fact, most brands contain nicotine. Or she may think that the nicotine content is acceptably low, unaware there are other harmful chemicals. If you say it can lead to other addictions, she may say you are old-fashioned and ill-informed.

⊚ **She may vape** to banish hunger pangs to try to lose weight.

⊚ **She may enjoy** "cloud-chasing" (blowing vapor shapes) and comparing flavors with her friends.

MANY TEENS DON'T FULLY UNDERSTAND THE HEALTH IMPACT OF VAPING.

HOW YOU COULD RESPOND

In the moment

Get her perspective
Rather than bombard her with warnings, ask nonjudgmental questions to open up the conversation. Acknowledge the attraction. Say you don't want to stop her having fun, but you want to talk about the possible risks because you love her.

Help her weigh the evidence
If you say that e-cigarettes are as harmful as normal ones, she'll stop listening. Accept that compared to traditional cigarettes, there seem to be fewer risks, but ask her to check other evidence. Suggest she watches online talks from researchers weighing possible risks. Mention side effects such as gum disease and bad breath.

Talk about other unknowns
Mention possible harm from chemicals in the aerosol. Tell her, "No one knew about the dangers of cigarettes. It took years for diseases to develop for doctors to work out a link."

In the long term

Point out that teens are targeted
Teens want to be free of adult control. Explain how firms target them using social media influencers. Many vaping products are made by firms that make tobacco cigarettes. Say that once addicted, you lose your freedom of choice.

State your expectations
Tell her that while ultimately it's her choice, you hope that she'll stop for the sake of her health.

Talk about the cost
Using spending cash on vaping means she won't have money for other things. Say you might consider putting half her allowance in a savings account so she doesn't waste it.

Help her address underlying causes
If she's vaping to distract from anxiety or depression, address these. Suggest cognitive behavioral therapy to help her deal with worries or cravings.

"I'M WORRIED ABOUT
THE FUTURE."

Now that your teen is reaching adulthood, she's thinking more about how her future will look. Beyond worrying about choosing the right career and finding a partner, she may also be anxious about how much the world itself is going to change in the years to come.

SCENARIO | While watching the news, your teen says she worries about how her future will be affected by issues such as climate change.

Just a couple of years ago, your teen will have imagined a future of fun and freedom. Now that she's almost independent, she'll be thinking more practically about the realities of adult life. As well as the usual worries about her career, owning a home, and relationships, larger concerns about issues such as climate change, overpopulation, and economic and political uncertainty may make her feel like she can't take a safe future for granted. If she seems overwhelmed, she's likely to be using "emotional thinking," whereby her feelings of hopelessness become a belief that things will never improve.

WHAT YOU MIGHT BE THINKING

You may be secretly worried, too, that she's entering an uncertain world. You may wonder what you can say or do to reassure her when you're also scared of what the future will hold or whether it will even be safe for her to have children of her own.

WHAT SHE MIGHT BE THINKING

⊙ **Your teen's fear** of the unknown may be creating high levels of anxiety now, making it harder for her to concentrate on her work or relax.

⊙ **If you try to reassure** her with trite phrases, she may believe you're dismissing her worries. If you haven't adapted your own lifestyle to be greener, she may feel more alone and see you as part of the problem.

⊙ **Your teen may be angry** that she's facing an uncertainty she didn't create and frustrated that political and ecological decisions made by older people are affecting her future.

⊙ **To develop her motivation**, your teen needs to be able to visualize her goals, whether it's working toward a career or owning her first home. If she feels she has nothing to work for, this may impact how hard she works toward these things.

SEE RELATED TOPICS
Anxiety and depression: pp.188–189
I miss you: pp.206–207

" "
AS ADULT LIFE BECKONS, YOUR TEEN MAY BEGIN TO WORRY ABOUT BROADER ISSUES.

HOW YOU COULD RESPOND

In the moment

Step back and listen
Though it may be upsetting to hear her concerns, having an open conversation will help calm her anxiety. Tell her that her feelings make sense in uncertain times and are also a natural part of her transition to adulthood.

Talk about worry being positive
Tell her that her concern is a healthy, natural response to events, which will inspire her—and a growing number of others—to act to limit environmental damage.

Discuss how to help
Research shows that teens who are concerned yet optimistic do the most to look after the planet. Encourage her to channel her anxiety into helping make a difference, whether it's cutting her use of plastic, no longer eating meat, or reducing her carbon footprint in other ways. This will help give her a sense of control over her life. Show that you're also willing to make changes so she doesn't feel isolated in her concerns.

In the long term

Help her live in the moment
Rather than fret unnecessarily about events that may not occur, tell her the future has yet to arrive and it's good to live in the "now."

Get her outside
The environment can feel like an abstract idea from indoors. Suggest she gets out to do something locally, such as help plant trees or pick up plastic. Time in nature also reduces feelings of stress.

Help her to self-calm
If stress levels stay high for long periods, they can block well-being neurochemicals such as serotonin (a mood stabilizer) and oxytocin, which give a sense of "all's well." Encourage daily relaxation time, whether it's a few minutes reading a book—found to relieve stress in the moment by 68 percent—exercising, or meditating. This self-care will equip her to deal better with bigger challenges.

"SORRY YOU HAVEN'T HEARD FROM ME."

When your teen leaves for college, it can feel like the end of her childhood for both of you. While she may be enjoying a new sense of independence now, as a parent, you may be feeling a deep sense of loss, especially if she doesn't stay in touch as much as you'd hoped.

SCENARIO | Two weeks into term, your teen texts to apologize for not being in touch.

While your teen is off on a big adventure, you're left behind in a home that's full of constant reminders of her. After 18 years of close involvement, you're now having to get used to knowing less about her life, where she is, and who she's with—and you may feel like an outsider looking in, extraneous to her needs. While she may just be busy and overwhelmed with all the new experiences college life offers, her lack of contact may also be a subtle way of saying she's enjoying her privacy and would now like to be seen more as an adult than a child.

WHAT YOU MIGHT BE THINKING

You may feel hurt it's taken her so long to get in touch. You want her to settle in, but may feel rejected if she doesn't seem to need you. You may wonder if this is what your relationship will be like now.

WHAT SHE MIGHT BE THINKING

⊙ **Teens are naturally** self-centered, so she may find it liberating to think only about herself. She may also want to prove she's capable of coping in the adult world.

⊙ **If she wants to keep** parts of her new life private, she may be avoiding a conversation if she fears you'll pry. However, the longer she's left getting in touch, the more guilty she feels, and the more worried you might be angry.

⊙ **If she's usually communicative**, she may be trying to hide the fact that she is not yet enjoying college or is lonely. Or if she thinks you've been too involved or invested in her success to date, she may want to distance herself now.

SEE RELATED TOPICS
I'm taking a year off: pp.190–191
I miss you: pp.206–207

HOW YOU COULD RESPOND

In the moment

Allow yourself time to adjust
After being tied up in her daily life for the last 18 years, it will take time to get used to her absence. Think of how you can channel your energy and return to interests and outlets you've neglected since becoming a parent.

See it as a positive
If you have a good relationship with her, view her independence as a sign she's securely attached to you and you've prepared her well for adulthood. Avoid making her feel responsible for your feelings of loss.

Look after your partnership
If you have a co-parent, discuss how much you've achieved together and contributed to the successful development of your child. Try to understand how each of you feels about her departure to help you reconnect, and talk about how you want the next stage of your lives to look.

In the long term

See it as a phase
She's likely to be negotiating a more adult relationship with you as part of the separation process and may be more distant while she proves she can survive without you.

Let her get in touch
Students report they're happier when they initiate contact rather than feel pursued by parents. Let her know you're there when she needs you and keep her posted on what's happening at home, even if you don't get a reply.

Try more casual communication
Set up a family chat group where you can all post pictures and conversations. Send her the occasional GIF, making it clear you are thinking of her but don't always need a response. Feel free to send letters or care packages, too. Students report this helps them feel cared about without being too intrusive.

INDEX

THE AUTHOR

Tanith Carey is a parenting writer and award-winning journalist. She is the author of 10 parenting books, which analyze some of the most urgent issues for today's parents and offer practical, research-based solutions. Tanith's books have been translated into 20 languages, including Spanish, French, Italian, German, and Arabic and have received widespread global media coverage. Her books include *What's My Child Thinking?*, *The Friendship Maze*, *Taming the Tiger Parent*, and *Girls Uninterrupted: Steps for Building Stronger Girls in a Challenging World*. Tanith's speaking engagements have included the Child Mind Institute in Palo Alto, California, and The Cheltenham Science Festival. She is a regular contributor to TV and radio programs, including the *Today Show* on NBC and BBC Radio Four's *Woman's Hour*. Tanith has two daughters, age 18 and 15. For a full biography, see www.tanithcarey.com.

THE CONSULTANTS

Dr. Carl Pickhardt is a Harvard University–educated counselor and psychologist with 30 years of experience working with parents and adolescents. He is the author of the popular *Psychology Today* blog "Surviving (Your Child's) Adolescence." Dr. Pickhardt is a seasoned public speaker and the author of several books, including *Who Stole My Child?* (2018), a guide to parenting through the stages of adolescence. He has four children and three grandchildren.

Dr. Angharad Rudkin is a Clinical Psychologist and Associate Fellow of the British Psychological Society. She has worked with children, adolescents, and families for 20 years. Angharad has an independent therapy practice and teaches Clinical Child Psychology at the University of Southampton. She regularly contributes to articles on child and family well-being for national newspapers and magazines and is a relationship expert for London's *Metro* daily newspaper. Angharad appears on TV and radio regularly as an expert on child and family issues.

ACKNOWLEDGMENTS

From Tanith Carey Thanks to my children Lily and Clio, who have always been my inspiration. Also love to my husband Anthony, whose support has allowed me to take the time to write this book. As always, the process of writing the book has been made so much easier by working with Dr. Angharad Rudkin. Thanks must also go to the highly professional team at DK, in particular my editor Claire Cross and commissioning editor Dawn Henderson.

From Dr. Rudkin Thank you to all the families and young people I have worked with over the last 20 years. I have learned so much from you all and never fail to be amazed at your courage. It has been an enormous pleasure to work with Tanith again, who finds such clarity in the midst of complex issues. Many thanks also to the DK team, including Claire Cross. Finally, a heartfelt thank you to all of my family, who have helped me make sense of the world from the very start.

From the Publisher We would like to acknowledge the following in the production of this book: Claire Wedderburn-Maxwell for proofreading and Vanessa Bird for indexing.

To access the research and studies supporting the text in this book, visit:
www.dk.com/wmtt-biblio